If Augustine Were Alive

If Augustine Were Alive

AUGUSTINE'S RELIGIOUS IDEAL FOR TODAY

by

THEODORE TACK, O.S.A.

ALBA · HOUSE NEW · YORK

SOCIETY OF ST. PAUL, 2187 VICTORY BLVD., STATEN ISLAND, NEW YORK 10314

Library of Congress Cataloging-in-Publication Data

Tack, Theodore.
    If Augustine were alive.

    Bibliography: p.
    1. Augustine, Saint, Bishop of Hippo.   2. Christian
life — Early church, ca. 30-600.   I. Title.
BR65.A9T33   1988   248'.092'4   88-16825
ISBN 0-8189-0539-5

Designed, printed and bound in the United States of
America by the Fathers and Brothers of the
Society of St. Paul, 2187 Victory Boulevard,
Staten Island, New York 10314, as part of their
communications apostolate.

Printing Information:

Current Printing - first digit   1   2   3   4   5   6   7   8   9   10   11   12   13   14   15   16   17   18   19   20

Year of Current Printing - first year shown

1988   1989   1990   1991   1992   1993   1994   1995   1996   1997   1998   1999   2000   2001   2002

CONTENTS

INTRODUCTION

S T. AUGUSTINE was truly a remarkable person. Over sixteen centuries have passed since his birth in 354 A.D. and his conversion to the Catholic faith in 386. Though he was well known in the Church of his own times, he is even better known and certainly more widely read today. There were those who disagreed with him when he was a bishop in North Africa — Pelagius, for example, was one of his more intellectual adversaries — and there are those who have disagreed with him and various aspects of his teaching in the centuries that have followed, including our own. But the Church as a whole has given great credence to this brilliant, insightful and very personable man, both during his lifetime and down through the centuries.

As a matter of fact, his influence is perhaps more forcefully felt now than in former times. One has only to think of the way he was cited, both explicitly and implicitly, by the Fathers of the Second Vatican Council to understand this point. He is also one of the most written-about authors in the world today. For the past several decades several hundred articles and books have been published about him and his works on a yearly basis. At least one of his books, his *Confessions*, has been translated into almost every modern language in the world and is still widely circulated. In many respects this book could be considered a "best seller," probably the best-selling book ever after the Bible.

What is it about this man who lived such a long time ago that still appeals to people today? His theological and philosophical genius are beyond question, it is true. But I would suggest that he still appeals to a lot of people today because he was so fully human, in the best sense of the word. He gives us valuable psychological insights into ourselves; his own personal odyssey is that of so many of us; his thirst for God and the difficulties he experienced in finding and holding on to God relate to a basic human need. Furthermore, the problems he faced in his own day are very similar to those we must face. Social upheaval marked his times as it does ours. Strong change was in the wind in the early fifth century, and no one could see where it would lead or where it would end. On the other hand he bared his soul, his mind, his feelings and his Christian heritage in such a way that people who are honest with themselves can still find in Augustine some reflection of their own inner life and struggle.

Augustine also had some very keen insights into the Christian life itself, and what he frequently emphasized to his people, especially to consecrated Christians, are the very points which many religious families tend to accentuate today. Augustine strongly promoted a deep sense of Christian community, a common search for and praise of God, genuine friendship, and true respect for the individual, even while living in community. He encouraged others to a deep interior life and a restless pursuit of wisdom and truth. He was convinced they would find God precisely through this pursuit. Above all he wanted them to find and serve Christ in one another through a wholly practical mutual service and love. Leadership in the Church was to be based more upon love than on fear. In all this he emphasized the dignity and intrinsic value of the human person in a social milieu, a theme which is constantly being stressed in our own day and age.

The chapters of this book are concerned precisely with these and other similar points, and though they are principally addressed to those Christians who have consecrated themselves in community life to the service of others, either in the active or contemplative apostolates, I believe that they can well serve all Christians who wish to draw closer to the Lord. As a matter of fact, many of the examples that I have drawn from Augustine were originally addressed to all his people, as he spoke to them in a very familiar way in his cathedral church.

Pope Paul VI was a great admirer of St. Augustine. He once told a general audience in Rome that he tried to read at least one page of Augustine every day. On another occasion he remarked that, if Augustine were alive today, he would speak just as he had a thousand and more years ago, because he personifies a humanity that believes and loves Christ and God (Nov. 3, 1973). From this thought has come the title of this book.

Our present Holy Father's admiration for Augustine is no less evident. John Paul II quotes Augustine extensively in his writings and homilies. Moreover, he issued a lengthy Apostolic Letter on the occasion of the Sixteenth Century of Augustine's conversion (1986), in which he also speaks of what Augustine has to say to us today.

I have cited Augustine frequently in the chapters of this book, precisely because I too believe he has so much to say to our generation. Quite truthfully, that is also the way the vast majority of the retreatants have felt, to whom I originally offered these reflections over the past four years as part of a retreat program. It was their enthusiasm for Augustine and their encouragement that have now led me to offer these ideas to a broader audience.

In translating Augustine's thought into modern English I have tried to employ universal language where this was possible. Sometimes, however, such a translation did not fit the circumstances, as Augustine would be addressing himself to specific groups of men or women. Though Augustine's *Rule* is to be found in both a masculine and feminine version, for continuity and convenience's sake I have used only the masculine translation. The feminine form is exactly the same, except for a change in the respective pronominal forms.

In concluding his *Rule* Augustine tells his readers how he hopes it will serve as a mirror in which they can see themselves. I do not pretend so much, but I do hope that these reflections may serve as a source of encouragement and challenge for all who wish to draw closer to Christ.

AUGUSTINE'S RELIGIOUS IDEAL
FOR TODAY

1

COMMUNITY LIFE:
The Augustinian Experience

FROM HIS EARLIEST DAYS Augustine yearned for friends and found great strength and solace in them. They too were attracted to him by his warm and appealing personality.[1] In the light of this it is not difficult to understand how, even before his conversion, Augustine and his friends would come to propose the formation of a certain type of community among themselves. What they had in mind was perhaps what we would call a "philosophical" community, a community, that is, given over to the search for wisdom through individual reflection and common sharing. But still it was to have been a real community. As Augustine himself tells us, it was to have embraced separation from the crowd, a common fund for all possessions, and such a sharing of responsibilities that the majority would be free from having to concern themselves with material matters. The project collapsed, however, when they came to understand that their women would never agree to it.[2]

What is most interesting in all this is that, at the time, Augustine knew absolutely nothing about the monastic life as it then existed in the Church. It was a revelation and a source of amazement for him and his very close friend, Alypius, when their fellow-countryman from Africa, Ponticianus, told them about an Egyptian monk named Anthony, about certain monasteries flourishing in the desert, and about one monastery in particular right there in Milan, where Augustine was then living.[3] Ponticianus' narrative affected Augustine profoundly. It really marked the turning point in his life, though he had been slowly building toward this moment for years.

He was so moved by what Ponticianus had said that, after the visitor had departed, he dashed into the garden of the house where he and Alypius were living in order to be alone with himself. After suffering there the agonies of being further torn interiorly between two conflicting parts of himself, the grace of God finally prevailed and he was able to turn himself wholeheartedly to the Lord.[4]   It was early August of the year 386. During the following six months or so, which preceded his baptism, Augustine lived a kind of community experience in Cassiciacum, a small country village some 30 miles north of Milan. Though quite a bit of family was involved in this community — his mother Monica, his son Adeodatus, his good friend Alypius, and several other relatives, friends and students — perhaps we could speak of this as the very first "Augustinian" community.[5]

Augustine's Religious Ideal

After Monica's unforeseen death in the early autumn of 387 in the seaport of Ostia, Augustine spent the better part of a year in nearby Rome. During that time he visited various religious communities in and around the city and learned more about other monasteries existing elsewhere.[6] It must have been during this time that the idea matured in his mind about the kind of religious community he wanted for himself and his friends when he returned to Africa.

Possidius, Augustine's great friend, fellow bishop and principal early biographer, tells us that Augustine actually did found that first religious community in his home town of Tagaste (Souk Ahras in present-day Algeria), most probably in the autumn of the year 388, shortly after he had returned to Africa from Rome. There, together with some friends and fellow citizens, all of whom were laymen like himself, he lived in common, fasting, praying, performing good works and meditating constantly on the Word of God.[7] We know very little more about this first Augustinian religious community. This situation continued for approximately three years, until in late 391 Augustine was ordained a priest and founded his second monastery, this time in the seaport of Hippo (present-day Annaba, Algeria) near the church, in a garden given him by his bishop, Valerius. Possidius remarks that the style of life of this new Augustinian community was modeled after the early Christian community of Apostolic times,[8] but as he goes on to say, this was nothing new: Augustine had already established just such an apostolic manner of living in his first monastery, in Tagaste, *"when he had returned home across the sea."*[9]

Origins of the Rule of St. Augustine

Though there are some scholars who disagree, there is a strong opinion which holds that the *Rule*[10] of St. Augustine for religious was written around the years 396-397, probably on the occasion of Augustine's taking over as bishop of Hippo after Valerius's death. At this time he decided to leave his first foundation in Hippo and set up a monastery for the clerics who would be living with him in the episcopal household. Why he left that first monastery in Hippo, he himself tells us: it would not be good for the bishop to live on there, he remarked, because he would have to be receiving people at all times of the day, and he did not want the peace and quiet of the brothers to be unduly disturbed by so many comings and goings.[11]

Augustine's desire to follow the ideal of the early Jerusalem community is clearly spelled out in that rule of life, written for his followers. It is interesting to note also that thirty years later, when he was 72 years of age, Augustine confirmed in a very solemn way in his cathedral church that this same ideal was still the accepted model for him and the brothers living with him. On that occasion he had the deacon Lazarus read the passage from the *Acts of the Apostles* (4:31-35), which describes that early Christian community:

> The place where they were gathered shook as they prayed. They were filled with the Holy Spirit and continued to speak God's word with confidence. The community of believers were of one heart and one mind. None of them ever claimed anything as his own; rather, everything was held in common. With power the apostles bore witness to the resurrection of the Lord Jesus, and great respect was paid to them all; nor was there anyone needy among them, for all who owned property or houses sold them and donated the proceeds. They used to lay them at the feet of the apostles to be distributed to every one according to his need.

Augustine himself then took the Scriptures from the deacon, read out loud the same passage again, and commented to the people gathered in the church in overflowing numbers: *"You have just heard what we aspire to. Pray that we may be able to live such a life."*[12]

The main object of Augustine's *Rule* is really very simple: the brothers/sisters are to live together in their religious house in a harmonious manner, and be one in mind and heart on their way to God.[13]   The one great demand, then, made of all those who would enter upon this style of religious life, was that they constantly strive to form a community in which everything would be clearly directed toward God, and where unanimity and concord would be emphasized. In a very few words, everything in the *Rule* points to forming a community of faith and love.

One of the striking characteritics of this community is that God is to be sought, encountered and possessed in and through the mutual love and concern of the brothers/sisters for one another. This very love and concern, unanimity and concord, constitute a real honoring of God in one's fellow religious: each one recognizes that the others are temples of God as much as they themselves, and indeed that together they also form but one temple of the Lord.[14]   Augustine sees the oneness of his religious culminating in their oneness with Christ: *"They are not many souls, but only one, the one soul of Christ."*[15]   One Augustinian scholar even goes so far as to say that living the common life as Augustine spells it out constitutes in itself one's *"primary worship of God."*[16]   From this point of view it would seem that the mutual love and service of one another take on a quasi-liturgical aspect, a true public honoring of God present in the person of the other. This simple idea gives a new and very profound dimension to living together in community, one which could certainly transform many communities and even the very lives of those living together, were it to be better understood and more fully emphasized.

Unity in Love through Community

If you search the original Latin text of the *Rule* for the word "community", you will find it explicitly only once.[17]   Yet the concept of community pervades every aspect of that *Rule*. Everything in it is other-directed, aimed toward making possible what

Augustine has laid down as the first purpose to be realized in the religious life. Many situations which Augustine describes and much of the advice which he gives in this little booklet are directed toward this chief goal. God is truly loved and honored through the concrete service religious offer one another. These small details of life, and especially the interior attitude which accompanies them, are precisely what tend to make the many become one, just as the Father and Jesus are one.[18]

Moreover, the master principle of unity which lies behind all these details and brings all the diverse facets of the Augustinian community together is none other than love. Augustine even declares that religious will make progress in love insofar as they show a greater concern for the common good than for their own advantage.[19] This same insistence on fraternal love as the measuring stick of progress fits in well with the awe Augustine experiences in the face of the Lord's description of the last judgment. There, the eternal happiness of the blessed is seen to depend on the love they have shown to their brothers and sisters who are in need, a service which is characterized on the one hand by real selflessness, and on the other by true considerateness for those who are God's little ones. The question that quite naturally comes up here is simply this: Are not those who have given up everything to embrace the religious life especially to be numbered among these blessed because of the selfless service and considerateness they have shown to others, beginning with their fellow religious in the community? That certainly seems to be the mind of Augustine.[20]

Sharing and Caring in the Rule

Consider for a moment how such selflessness and considerateness, mutual encouragement and understanding, sharing and caring show up in the following themes and ideas taken from the *Rule*:

1) All the religious are to receive according to their particular needs and are to share cheerfully what they have or may receive as gifts. Humility — which allows people to see themselves as they really are in God's sight and accept one another's differences — is to be their constant guide, no matter what condition of life they may have come from, for in the community all have a common goal: living in harmony with one another to the extent of becoming one in the one Christ.[21]

2) All the members of the community are called together for common prayer at fixed times, but if some want to pray in their free time, the others are to support them, at least by being considerate enough not to disturb their prayer.[22]

3) The religious are expected to be understanding when for a good reason special food or clothing is given to some and not to others.[23]

4) The sick are to be the object of special care by the community, and one religious in particular is to be delegated to see that the sick are properly taken care of.[24]

5) While chastity is a very personal offering to God, Augustine alerts the community to be aware of its own responsibility in this matter, telling all to exercise a mutual care and vigilance over one another, because in this way *"God who dwells in you will grant you his protection."* Once again the idea of the presence of God in the individual religious and in the community is emphasized as a stimulus for supporting their mutual consecration in a practical way.[25]

6) In much the same way, fraternal correction becomes a sign of caring love. Those who fail to admonish one who is in danger not only do that person a great disservice, but also share in the total blame, and fall short in their love both for the person and for the community.[26]

7) All one's work is to be accomplished for the common good, not for one's personal benefit.[27]

8) When the religious go out, they lend one another mutual support by going together.[28]

9) Anyone who offends another is expected to ask pardon and to receive forgiveness as soon as possible, because there can be no harmony or concord where open wounds are allowed to fester.[29]

10) Finally, obedience is necessary, not only because God dwells in the superior, but also because it is a way of showing mercy and compassion to that religious and to the entire community. Indeed, it is the community which is injured by those who fail to obey, because such as these place their own will and advantage ahead of the common good.[30]

In all this we can see that the Augustinian-oriented community has at one and the same time both a spiritual reality, namely, the common search for God, which is its principal goal; and a true human reality, that is, the building up of a loving, welcoming, supportive, caring and challenging fraternity. These two realities — the spiritual and the human — are fused into one by Augustine's insistence that the religious become more and more aware of the presence of God in one another. As this awareness grows, the search for God and the building up of the fraternity become a single, common effort. This community thrust also goes contrary to all that favors the self: personal possessions, power, pride, independence, competition, egoism — elements which often characterize relationships in secular society and which, unfortunately, are sometimes even considered the hallmark of progress and achievement in society. One of Augustine's sayings sums up very well the emphasis he places on the love of one's brothers or sisters in the community as the culmination of their effort to love God:

Are they perfect who know how to live together? They are perfect who fulfill the law. But how is the law of Christ fulfilled by those who live together as brothers and sisters? Listen to the Apostle: *"Bear one another's burdens: This is how you will fulfill the law of Christ"* (Gal 6:2).[31]

Throughout the *Rule*, the followers of Augustine are asked to bear their brothers's and sister's burdens as though they were their own. In this way they will be able to know that they are really imitating Christ and his love.

The Central Place of Community Life

Those who have written about the type of life described by Augustine in his *Rule* have always emphasized the central place of the community in this life. Moreover, they point out this centrality as something very characteristic of Augustine's approach to the religious life. A few examples from some modern authors will help illustrate this point.

But for Augustine the common life is more than just a means. It is in community that one may meet with God. He uses striking language: "Whoever is willing to live under one roof with me has God for his possession" . . . One can find no other legislation in which the notion of community has so consciously and forcefully been made the central point of all monastic living. . . To be a family of God, to be a community of love, and in that community to strive for the perfect realization of the ideals of Christian life — that is the thought at the heart of all that Augustine did in establishing his form of monastic life.[32]

Why is there such a strong emphasis on community? Would it not be because a tendency to favor one's ego and individualism are the principal obstacles to living the Gospel? . . . [Augustine's vision of community] is a protest against indifference towards people and the' lack of equality among them, such as we find so frequently in society.[33]

The only condition that Augustine placed on Bishop Valerius when he was ordained a priest was that he be able to continue living in community. And the only thing that he always insisted on as he adapted to the different apostolic needs of the Church was community . His entire apostolic activity was based on community life.[34]

These expressions, which lay bare the fundamental importance of a person-oriented community life in the Augustinian religious ideal, provide good reason to pause and reflect on what such a life can and should be. One who lives in such a style of community and strives for the ideal proposed already possesses God and offers to others a model of what the real Christian ideal is, a model which serves not only for other religious, but perhaps especially for all Christian families. In looking out for others before oneself, the religious offers a sign of protest against both the priorities which the world has set for itself and the terrible pain of loneliness and abandonment which so many people experience in our computerized society. In listening to the Gospel with the other members of the community, the religious are declaring that no one alone possesses the whole truth, and that Jesus still speaks and teaches when two or three are gathered in his name. Moreover, even though we may learn many things from others, it is Jesus who is the real interior Master, and therefore our constant guide and ultimate spiritual director.[35]   Finally, Augustine's religious lifestyle is not something apart from the mainstream of the Church, but is rather the foundation of all apostolic service and a true reflection of that unity of love in Christ, which should characterize all Christians.

Summing Up

To sum up briefly, the central place of the community in Augustine's view and experience of religious life comes through quite clearly: 1) In this community God is to be sought, possessed and honored in a very concrete way, in and through one's fellow religious. 2) Community life thus lived is an act of worship of God. 3) The entire *Rule* is other-directed: it urges a sharing and caring which lead to unanimity and concord; furthermore, progress in love is measured by the degree in which the common good is sought before one's own. 4) Finally, such a community rules out all forms of selfishness, for selfishness is the major obstacle to a Gospel view of life and to following Jesus. The centrality of living the common life is so accentuated in Augustine's thought that the vows of chastity, poverty and obedience as we know them today could well be said to be contained in the one, so-called 'holy commitment,' which Augustine demanded of all who would join his way of life. This 'holy commitment' is none other than the proposal to live the common life in unanimity of purpose and in concord among all.[36]   Religious who take this 'holy commitment' seriously will not only be pleasing to God, but will also be a source of great joy for the other members of the community, as well as for the Church itself.

2

LET EVERYTHING BE YOURS IN COMMON

IN OUR WORLD TODAY there is an abundance of material goods in certain countries. In others — the majority, without doubt — countless of God's people live in poverty or even abject misery. In this context the entire question of religious poverty becomes a very challenging one. If what religious share with others is to be meaningful, this offering must come from within, from an interior life that is inspired by love. This is the very purpose of religious vows: they must help deepen one's love for God and neighbor. The vow of religious poverty takes on real meaning only when viewed in the broader context of a life dedicated to union with Christ and generous service of one's neighbor. Outside of this or a similar context, this vow would not make sense and could easily be construed as totally undesirable.

Just such a broader picture of the Augustinian religious ideal has already been sketched in the preceding chapter. To sum this up very briefly: the fundamental purpose of life together in an Augustinian-oriented community is the achievement of harmony and unity among the religious in their search for God, a goal which should result first of all from finding God in one another — and honoring him there.[1]   In this way the Christ becomes visible and palpable: he can be effectively loved and served in his weak humanity, the weak humanity, that is, of each one of us. It is in this light that we must view and evaluate Augustine's strong insistence on evangelical poverty, or better, his insistence on the total sharing of goods in the religious community.

Augustine was very much aware of the importance of this total sharing from the moment he began to live the religious life himself. He well understood that true unity and harmony among his followers would not be possible if they were to be able to possess what they wished and use these things as they wished. As Augustine put it on one occasion:

> On account of those things which we possess as individuals, quarrels arise, enmities, dissensions, wars among men, uprisings, disagreements. . . . Do we fight about those things we hold in common?[2]

But if the ultimate purpose of religious poverty, or sharing, is clear for Augustine, what was his mind concerning the content and practice of this poverty? I would like to sum up his attitude under four main headings: *sharing, receiving, living, serving.*

1. SHARING WITH THE COMMUNITY

The basic principle which Augustine sets down for religious in this matter is to be found at the very beginning of his *Rule: "Call nothing your own, but let everything be yours in common."*[3]   This implies first of all that when people come to an Augustinian-oriented community they do as Augustine did, giving what they have to the poor or adding it to the common store of the religious community. In this regard Augustine says:

> Let them do as they wish. As long as they remain paupers with me, we all may hope for the mercy of God.[4]

This basic principle of total sharing, however, also makes it clear that, though religious are to have nothing of their own, everything is to be theirs in common with the other brothers or sisters. Before entering the religious life only their personal possessions could be claimed as their own. After entering this holy society and putting all in common, even what the others had would now belong to each one.[5]   What is even more remarkable is the fact that God himself thus becomes the common and most prized possession of all: *"Indeed, God himself, that great and superabundant treasure, will be our common possession."*[6]

This basic norm, however, did not concern only those who were just entering upon their holy commitment as consecrated Christians. It also applied to those who were already living the common life. All, for example, who received gifts from out-siders, even from relatives, were expected to put these things in common; it would then be up to the superior to see that these gifts were given to whoever might need them. Moreover, Augustine even made it clear to the people of his diocese that, if he were to consider some gifts they gave him as being too elegant, he would sell the object and use the money for some charitable purpose, rather than wear or use what was unbecom-ing to his religious profession.[7]   It is precisely by means of this attitude that Augustine teaches religious even today the need for simplicity: some things are simply not suited for those who profess to be among the poor of Christ.

But perhaps the most important detail of this total sharing

with the community was the positive attitude which Augustine
wanted to see present in those who came to live with him:
cheerfulness in giving on the part of those who had possessions in
the world;[8]   the *absence of a desire to acquire things* on the part of
those who came to the community without having possessed
material goods.[9]   Cheerfulness, moreover, was to characterize
all who lived in the monastery through the services they
rendered to one another,[10]   and in their very manner of observing the *Rule*, that is, *as those living in freedom under grace.*[11]
Augustine also underlined how the absence of a longing to
possess things rendered the religious' self-offering a total
sacrifice: *"That person gives up the entire world who gives up what
he/she possesses and desires to possess."*[12]   Nevertheless, what
really counts is not whether people have brought something to
the common store or sold all they had. Rather it is that they have
brought with them to the community that *"charity which out-
shines all things. . . ."*[13]

2. RECEIVING IN KEEPING WITH EACH ONE'S NEEDS

The second norm concerning poverty, which is set down
by Augustine for his followers, is taken directly from the manner
of living described in the early Jerusalem community: distribu-
tion of goods is to be made to each one according to each one's
need.[14]   Unity, not uniformity is the goal of Augustinian poverty. The real differences among religious, such as health,
strength, background, talents and other personal needs, must be
taken into consideration at all times.

In making provision for such differences in his *Rule*
Augustine showed how broad-minded he was, how considerate
of what made people different from one another. He understood
that the needs of those who were formerly rich were bound to be

distinct from those who had lived in poverty; that the needs of the healthy would be distinct from those who were sick; and that the strong would not need as much as the weak. He took into account in his religious not only their physical condition, but also their spiritual maturity and their psychological state — all of which showed an extraordinary understanding of human nature for the times he lived in. In this way he provided particular rules for the sick regarding fasting and taking nourishment;[15] special food, clothing and bedding were to be given to those whose background in the world made them less able to adapt quickly to monastic austerity;[16]   and though he admonished his followers not to be too concerned about what they were given to wear from the common store, he also made allowances for those who could not yet adapt themselves to this counsel.[17]

3. LIVING AS THOSE WHO ARE POOR IN SPIRIT

We have seen how Augustine wanted his followers to be poor in fact. But just how poor did he expect them to be in spirit, interiorly? What was the spirit that guided Augustine and his early communities in the daily living of their consecration as poor men of God?

To begin to provide an answer to these questions, we should first of all listen to Augustine as he tells the Christian people who, in his estimation, are God's poor, or the poor in spirit:

> A poor man of God is . . . one who is so in his heart, not in his pocketbook. . . . God does not look into our pockets but into our desires. . . . All those who are humble of heart, who live in the practice of the twofold commandment of love, no matter what they possess in this world, are always to be classified as the poor, those very poor whom God fills with bread.[18]

> See how the poor and the deprived belong to God, but of course
> I am speaking of the poor in spirit. Of these, indeed, is the
> kingdom of heaven. . . . And who are these poor in spirit? The
> humble, those who confess their sins, do not presume on their own
> merits or on their own justification. . . . Those who praise God when
> they do something good, and accuse themselves if they do something
> wrong.[19]

It is striking to see how in these texts Augustine brings
together the concepts of the poor in spirit and the humble of
heart: for him these concepts are inseparable. For Augustine it
would be utopian for people to seek unity and harmony on their
way to God without the practice of both these virtues. Furthermore, Augustine stresses that the poor of God and the poor in
spirit are likewise the humble of heart, and as such they necessarily practice the love of God and neighbor. At the same time he
was not taken in by some who made a display of giving their
wealth to the poor, but who were not themselves disposed to
become the poor of God:

> They are puffed up with pride and think that the good life they lead
> is attributable to themselves, not to the grace of God. Therefore,
> even though they accomplish many good works, they do not live
> well. . . . Their wealth is themselves, they are not the poor of God.
> They are full of themselves, not in need of God.[20]

The truly poor, therefore, will be so first of all in their
hearts: in all humility they will recognize both their need to be
filled by God and the fact that without God they will not be able
to accomplish anything worthwhile for the kingdom. Now these
concepts were first of all directed to all the faithful. Much more
must they concern religious.

Another point to be made in this area of living poverty on a
daily basis is that Augustine always sought to steer a middle
course. He did not believe in extremes. One part of the *Rule*,
which reveals such a balanced attitude concerning poverty,

regards the clothing the religious are to wear: *"There should be nothing about your clothing to attract attention."*[21]   No details are provided as to how this should be accomplished. The only thing counselled — and therefore what is most important for Augustine — is that the clothing be simple, neither too good nor too poor. In other words, it should not make them stand out in any way. This same kind of balanced attitude is expressed even more explicitly by Possidius, who gives us quite an insight into Augustine's personal living habits:

> His garments and footwear and even his bedroom furnishings were modest yet sufficient, neither too fine nor yet too mean. For in such things people are accustomed either to display themselves proudly or else to degrade themselves, in either case seeking not the things which are of Jesus Christ, but their own. But Augustine, as I have said, held a middle course, turning neither to the right nor to the left.[22]

One final point deserves to be made regarding the daily living of religious poverty: it concerns the need for religious to earn their livelihood by working. Augustine's entire book *On the Work of Religious* could be read and cited in this regard, but perhaps the following statement from this work adequately sums up his mind:

> Some have given up or distributed their great or mediocre fortune, and with salutary humility have wished to be numbered among the poor of Christ. If they are physically able, not engaged in ecclesiastical labors, and yet also do manual work, they take away all excuse [for not working] from those lazy people who come to the monastery from a more humble and therefore more active way of life. And in this way they act more mercifully than when they distributed all their goods to the needy.[23]

Religious cannot say that they are properly living the vow of poverty if they are not willing — insofar as health permits —

to take up cheerfully the burden of daily work, be it prayer, the pastoral ministry, teaching, writing, nursing, manual labor, technical services or any other form of the apostolate. If there is one thing that characterizes the truly poor, it is the fact that they must not only work, but work hard to sustain themselves and their families.

4. SERVING THOSE IN NEED

Finally, since it is clear that religious poverty is not simply an economic condition but an attitude of the heart based on love, its effects should also be felt beyond the walls of the religious community in an outgoing service to others. Jesus Christ emptied himself when he came among us: though abundantly rich, he became poor for our sake, so that through his poverty we ourselves might be enriched.[24]   This challenge is directed to all followers of Christ, and much more so to religious. It is a challenge to give oneself to God's little ones. Augustine fully understood and accepted this self-offering in his own day and was a model to his followers to go and do the same. As Possidius put it:

> He was always mindful of his companions in poverty. He gave
> to them by taking from what was set aside for his own use and that
> of those who lived with him, that is, the income from the goods of the
> church and the offerings of the faithful.[25]

> Sometimes when the church had no money, he informed the faithful that he had nothing more that he could give to the poor. In
> order to help prisoners and a great number of poor people, he had
> some sacred vessels broken up and melted down. What he then
> received from their sale, he distributed to the needy.[26]

But beyond these material cares for the companions of his poverty, as he was accustomed to call the poor, he also put himself out continually to help people through various works of mercy,[27]   for he well understood that one does not live on bread alone.[28]

In what ways, we may ask, can religious in particular imitate Augustine in his warm concern for the poor? One author offers a broad number of possibilities in the following statement:

> The religious has committed himself . . . to identify himself and his institute with the whole human family, inasmuch as it exhibits its poverty in manifold ways before God. In addition to the more obvious form of deprivation, the lack of material goods, there is the poverty of ignorance, of insecurity, of loneliness, of illness, of failure, above all, the poverty of sinfulness. By giving gratis and generously what he himself has received as gifts from God, the religious endeavors to carry out creatively the command of Jesus: 'You have received without paying: you must give without charge' (Mt 10:8).[29]

In this statement we can find a number of areas in which the poor of Christ can be better served in our world. But this service cannot be achieved without a real spirit of self-sacrifice, a willingness to put oneself out. Once again the challenge is laid down to live in that admirable simplicity which characterized Augustine's life, to experience deeply within ourselves the need for God and one another, and to hunger especially for God and the coming of his kingdom.

Augustine permits us to sum up his teaching on poverty in what constitutes the very heart of this matter: the real gift that is being asked of us through evangelical poverty is nothing less than the gift of self. Augustine brings this out in the following brief passage:

> Give what you promised; and since your promise concerns yourselves, give yourselves to the One who has given you exist- ence. . . . Whatever you give, far from being lessened, it will rather be preserved and increased.[30]

In the same vein, the goal of becoming one in mind and heart on their way to God will be even more quickly attained when religious share with others not only what they have but who they are, in other words, once again, the gift of self. When they share their talents of mind and heart, their faith, hope and love, their time, enthusiasm, and their very selves, then that proposed unity in love will become more attainable and more meaningful. The most important needs of men and women today are not necessarily material ones. Frequently their spiritual, psychological and emotional needs require greater and more immediate attention. The possibility of contributing something to alleviate these needs is probably more within the power of religious than that of relieving purely material needs.

Following the Poor Christ

Augustine challenges us to accept wholeheartedly, not only the giving up of our possessions for the poor, but also, in a very positive way, a meaningful following of Christ, who invites every religious: Come, follow me:

> Do you love, and do you wish to follow the one whom you love? He has hastened on, he has flown on ahead. Look and see where. O Christian! Don't you know where your Lord has gone? I ask you: Do you wish to follow him there? Through trials, insults, false accusations, through being spat upon in the face and slapped and beaten, through the crown of thorns, the cross and death? Why do you hesitate? Look, the way has been shown you. But, you say, it is a hard way. Who can follow him along it?[31]

Quite possibly not all these challenges will confront every religious in his or her lifetime. But the question still remains: *"Do you love, and do you wish to follow the one whom you love?"* In practice what does this mean?

Fr. Boniface Ramsey, O.P., in asking the same question, spells out several areas in which religious should be affected if they really wish to follow the one they love. To sum these up briefly, this means we should experience: 1) the emptiness of our human condition; 2) Christ's alienation from the standards set down by the rulers and society of his time; 3) his solidarity with the poor, the oppressed and the alienated; 4) his lack of power (or helplessness) in the face of certain situations; 5) his freedom with respect to human affairs; 6) his dependence on others and especially his total dependence on the Father.[32]

As an aid to a practical reflection on this matter, I would like to comment briefly on four key words or concepts which I find expressed here: *alienation, solidarity, helplessness, dependence.*

Alienation. The standards of our world are not those laid down by Jesus in the Gospel. Therefore, if we want to adhere to what Jesus teaches, we will have to distance ourselves from these standards. Consider, for instance, these two concrete examples: 1) the consumer mentality, which is constantly being thrust upon us in ads and on television: "Hurry, hurry! Buy it now! You can't possibly be happy without it!"; and 2) "If it doesn't make money, it can't be worthwhile!"

Let me give you a concrete example of how the consumer mentality preys on all, and perhaps especially on those who can least afford it. A few years ago I was on a central boulevard in Manila. While glancing around I was struck by a huge billboard set high above the street, but very visible to all passers-by. It showed the faces of three very sad looking children and proclaimed in bold letters: "How can you deprive your children of a color television set when it only costs $12.50 a month to rent one?" Of course the price was advertised in Philippine money, but it was the equivalent of about six or seven day's pay for the working class to whom it was directed. That billboard was proclaiming that sadness comes from not having a color TV; happiness is being able to enjoy one.

In an affluent society such as ours individuals and communities have to be very careful that they are not drawn to possess many material goods out of an exaggerated desire for comfort, or merely for the sake of possessing many things, or even out of a false competitive spirit. In the same way we have to be careful not to allow the real need for money in our work and life to so influence our outlook that we forget what is really important in the religious life, and maybe even stifle some of its essential elements: unity in love, community, prayer, service.

Solidarity.   We are rightly urged to practice solidarity with the poor. But this solidarity must not be limited to those who are only materially poor. As has been indicated above, it should also embrace the ignorant, the insecure, the lonely, the ill, those who suffer from failure, sinners.[33]   The whole area of justice and peace comes to mind here, an area that has been brought more and more to the forefront of our awareness in recent years. But as must be clear, we cannot attempt to speak out to others on this matter unless we have already set our own houses in order. Our whole attitude toward the under-privileged, the exceptional, minority groups, those who work for us or with us, needs to undergo close scrutiny, for it is precisely in this very personal area that the quest for greater justice in the world must begin. When we take this aspect of our lives seriously, then our solidarity with all the poor — even with those who may be materially wealthy — will take on a new and more significant meaning.

Helplessness.   Jesus experienced real helplessness many times during his life. He willingly submitted to this feeling because he wanted to be like us in all things except sin. He put up with a lot of uncertainties, frustrations, and anxieties, trusting throughout in the unfailing love of the Father. But we must ask here: Is there a similar willingness to put up with such things on the part of those religious — few in number, certainly — who seem to be suffering from what may be defined as a "rainy day" attitude? They are the kind who tend to stock up on the latest styles in clothing and gadgetry, who procure for themselves influential friends and other outside helps, not because they are interested in promoting the values of the kingdom or the needs of the community, but rather because of strictly personal interests. Behind this anxiety there seem to lie certain unspoken conditions, which have shaken the original generosity which was surely present when they began the religious life: "If I leave. . . ." or "If I can't accept my next assignment," or "If so-and-so becomes superior. . . ." Besides going against the basic tenets of the spirit of poverty, such attitudes display a basic unwillingness to trust in the Lord. If we aren't willing to trust the Lord and run prudent risks, how will we ever learn to deepen our love, which is the very goal of our lives together?

Dependence. Dependence can be experienced either with regard to others (the community) — and then it is perhaps better expressed as 'interdependence' — or with regard to the Lord himself. No one is asked to become so dependent on another that he or she is incapable of functioning alone. We all need a certain amount of autonomy in order to develop our talents and personalities to the best of our ability and in keeping with the needs of the Church and our religious Institute.

Here's a little story which shows very well the kind of dependence which we do not want to foster. During a recent summer vacation I found myself in one of our larger houses, where a farm is attached. We were praying Vespers one afternoon when a tremendous thunderstorm came up — and suddenly all the lights went out. The electricity was down for miles around. At that very moment a prize herd of cows was being milked in the barn, utilizing the very finest of modern machinery. When this machinery failed to work for lack of electricity, the cows refused to allow themselves to be milked the "old-fashioned" way, though this was tried. The result: the cows, swelling up with their milk, began to suffer so much that their "moo's" were heard all around the farm. They kept up their cries of pain till 3 o'clock in the morning, when the electricity was finally restored and they could be milked the modern way!

That's not the kind of dependence we want in the religious life. But if autonomy degenerates into independence, then the community is going to suffer. When someone can dispose of a large amount of money beyond what pastoral responsibilities require and has the unlimited use of a car, it is all too easy gradually to become independent of the community. In a similar way those who keep what comes to them from outside the community also effectively set themselves apart from others in the community, even though they may not realize it: possessing such items, especially in the case of money, makes them different, exempt as it were from some of the normal restrictions of community life. And strangely enough, though these people are unwilling to share with the community all they have received, they continue to want to have their share of everything the community offers its members. When I reflect on such an anomaly, I cannot help but call to mind the biblical scene of Ananias and Sapphira.[34]   This couple insisted they were giving all they had to the apostles, but they were really holding back. Perhaps they too suffered from that "rainy day" syndrome.

In the end, however, all manner of difficulties can be reduced to an unwillingness to accept dependence on the Lord, to trust him, seek him out and love him and all others in him. If some are intent on acquiring or possessing material things, it is hard to imagine how they will be intent upon God, will follow Jesus more closely, or will strive to love their fellow religious more generously. As Augustine puts it: *"That person is too greedy for whom God does not suffice."*[35]

In conclusion, it is well to recall that, for Augustine, sharing in common or professing evangelical poverty is just one more means — though an essential one — for fusing the members of a community into one, joining them all together as the *"one soul of Christ."*[36] The sacrifices necessary for living such an offering as evangelical poverty become acceptable when we keep the whole picture in mind, the very reason, that is, for which we have come together: to become one in mind and heart — in Christ — on our way to God.

3

TRUE FRIENDS IN CHRIST

UNTIL A RELATIVELY SHORT TIME ago the notion of friendship in the religious life easily stirred up feelings of apprehension and often aroused irrational fears. In fact it might have been considered imprudent or even unwise to write or speak about friendship in the positive light in which we now consider it. The only really acceptable use of the word seemed to occur in the context of highly spiritual, or "supernatural," relationships — the kind that were judged to have taken place between the saints down through the centuries. When writing on the topic of friendship, ascetical masters would often mention such spiritual friendships as being very admirable, but not always easy to achieve or keep free of dangerous sentimentality. They would then turn their attention to the evils of what have come to be known as "particular" friendships, relationships, that is, which in reality are exclusive, egoistical and divisive, and which also tend to become sensual. Very little space was dedicated to healthy intermediate levels of friendship.[1] Perhaps a certain, lingering, Jansenistic fear made us look for and expect the worst of fallen human nature.

'Innovations' at a General Chapter

Even after the Second Vatican Council it took some time for ideas to change. I remember well the 1968 Special General Chapter of the Augustinians, held on the campus of Villanova University in the U.S.A. — the first such Chapter ever held in the New World. This Special Chapter, as others held by all religious institutes in those years, had been mandated by the Holy See to renew the Constitutions of the Order. It was to be a clear response to Vatican II's urgent call for religious to return to their roots and to update their manner of living the religious life.[2]

The draft of these new Constitutions, as presented to the Chapter for consideration, had very specific references to the place of friendship in the Augustinian religious life. At the very beginning of the Chapter this fact triggered some severe criticism by a fair number of the Chapter members, who considered such notions as completely foreign to our way of life. In effect they were saying that the way we lived was based on a freely accepted juridical bond, and not on sentiments which, they felt, could change from one day to the next.

This criticism, however, paled when compared with the declarations of a few who considered as out of place in the Constitutions the new and broad concept of "fraternity" which was being introduced. In keeping with Vatican II this concept would have all of us be considered as true brothers, equal and deserving of the same respect, without regard for distinctions or privileges arising from special talents, university degrees, ordination or offices previously held. Thankfully, after long discussion and much prayer, fraternity and friendship prevailed and found their rightful place in the approved reform of the Constitutions. We Augustinians had indeed forgotten or neglected the marvelous heritage which we had received from St. Augustine. We, as so many other religious, had come to look down on a warmly human friendship in the religious life as suspect or dangerous, even though Augustine himself had considered friendship as one of the two most necessary things in the world![3]

No Fear of Friendship

Augustine had no fear of friendship or of making friends. Quite the contrary! Making friends was so ingrained in his nature that he could not conceive of himself living without them. This was the case both before and after his conversion to the Catholic faith.[4]   However, this does not imply that his ideas on friendship did not undergo some significant changes with his acceptance of faith in Jesus Christ and his entrance into the Catholic Church by baptism. Actually, his conversion led him to reflect that his earlier friendships had been to some degree defective, because they had not been cemented together by God, by that love which comes from the Holy Spirit.[5]

When he founded his first religious community in Tagaste, his first companions were some friends of long standing, along with a few other men of good will.[6]   Several of these followed him to Hippo three years later when he made his second foundation. Alypius, Evodius and Severus are the names of some of these friends who lived the religious life with him from the beginning; they were later joined by Possidius and others.[7] Augustine's friendship with these men was in no way diminished by his commitment to the Lord in the common life. Nor did it diminish, as later correspondence proves, when some of them left the community to answer the Church's call to become bishops. In fact, friendships with other clerics and laity, both men and women, multiplied during these same years.[8] We may truthfully say that not a few of his writings were inspired by the queries of his friends and at times by the ensuing dialogue with them.[9]

Augustine's manner of acting in this regard was certainly no different from what Jesus Christ himself taught and practiced in his own lifetime. Among his chosen twelve, as well as among his many other followers, Jesus too had special friends: John, the beloved disciple; Mary Magdalene; Mary, Martha and their brother Lazarus, and others. But though he had special friends, Jesus desired to extend his friendship to all men and women who would keep his twofold commandment of love.[10]   He stated that the greatest sign of love was to lay down one's life for one's friends.[11]   A clear indication that the disciples were his true friends was confirmed by his sharing with them the intimate secrets that his Father had shared with him.[12]   Moreover, Jesus' teaching and attitude fit in perfectly with the high esteem in which friends and friendship are held throughout the pages of the Old Testament.[13]

Despite changes of mentality and other kinds of growth since the end of the Second Vatican Council, some fears concerning friendship in religious life may still persist today, perhaps because in the wake of the Council a few exaggerations did appear in the name of a misguided or misunderstood friendship.[14]   Yet at the same time as there may have been some errors, these recent years have also seen great strides taken toward a better appreciation of the value and worth of the human person and of the meaning of true friendship in religious life.

An Augustinian View of Friendship

Augustine himself never wrote in a systematic way on friendship, even though, as already mentioned, this topic was very much a part of his life and thought. By drawing from his various writings we can briefly synthesize his thought on this matter in three main ideas: 1. *Friendship is essential* for a person's well-being in this world, but true friendship, which alone is lasting, only exists when it is inspired and welded together by God himself. 2. *Friendship presupposes love*, a true union of hearts, and a mutual sharing of burdens in the likeness of what Jesus did for us. 3. *Friendship is characterized by confidence and frankness*, and in its broadest interpretation is to be extended to all. Let's take a closer look at these basic ideas that help us appreciate how deeply Augustine felt about friendship, which was also very highly esteemed even by non-believers of ancient times.

1. WITHOUT A FRIEND, NOTHING IS FRIENDLY

In his own life Augustine experienced a great variety of friendships ranging from those that were very close, through those less involving emotionally, right down to an all-embracing, universal kind of relationship where no real distinction was made between friendship and fraternal love. He Christianized the classical, Ciceronian understanding of this virtue, showing that true friendship was a gift and special grace of God, faithfully kept only when lived in Christ. A few quotations can help clarify these points:

> Friendship cannot be true unless you [God] solder it together among those who cleave to one another by the charity poured forth in our hearts by the Holy Spirit.[15]

> You did not look down . . . on being the friend of the humble and returning the love that was shown to you. For what else is friendship but this? It gets its name from love alone, is faithful only in Christ, and in him alone can it be eternal and happy.[16]

> If together with me you hold firmly to these two commandments [the love of God and of one's neighbor], our friendship will be true and everlasting, and it will unite us not only to one another, but to the Lord himself.[17]

As one author puts it concerning these ideas of Augustine:

> This is the heart of Augustine's conception of friendship and his great innovation. It is God alone who can join two persons to each other. In other words, friendship is beyond the scope of human control. One can desire to be the friend of another who is striving for perfection, but only God can effect the union.[18]

Augustine is very clear concerning the fact that he himself simply could not live happily without friends. He needed and thrived on very warm, human relationships where common concerns, joys, sufferings, interests and ideas were shared fruitfully.[19] To Augustine's way of thinking there was no such thing as a purely spiritual friendship: by the very fact that friendship involves a return of love, it must extend to the whole person in his or her integral reality. Moreover, Augustine went far beyond indicating friendship as a personal necessity for himself alone. He saw friendship as a necessity for everyone. In fact he places health and friendship on the same plane, as special blessings of nature.[20] Just as God created us to exist and live in a healthful fashion, so did he also provide us with friendships so that we would not be alone in this life.[21] Precisely for this reason Augustine can conclude that without friends life is totally empty, even though one may enjoy the greatest riches and good health: "*Whenever a person is without a friend, not a single thing in the world appears friendly to him.*"[22] On the other hand, poverty, grief and pain itself can be accepted when there are good friends at hand to comfort and cheer us and to lighten our burden.

When we are weighed down by poverty and grief makes us sad; when bodily pain makes us restless and exile despondent, or when any other grievance afflicts us, if there be good people at hand who understand the art of rejoicing with the joyful and weeping with the sorrowful, who know how to speak a cheerful word and uplift us with their conversation, then bitterness is for the most part mitigated, worries are alleviated, and our troubles are overcome.[23]

Yet while *"there is no greater consolation than the unfeigned loyalty and mutual affection of good and true friends,"* in the midst of life's uncertainties we can experience real fear for their well-being. An even greater fear can arise from the realization that friends may fail us, perhaps even turn against us.[24]

2. LOVE: THE HEART OF FRIENDSHIP

Just as God works in people to make true friendship possible, this same friendship presupposes mutual love and a true union of hearts. Augustine frequently spoke of the hearts and souls of his friends and himself as being fused together in such a fashion that they were no longer many, but only one. Speaking of his dear friend Alypius, for example, he says: *"In body only, and not in soul, we are two, so great is the union of hearts, so firm the intimate friendship existing between us. . . ."*[25] Such unity, however, is only possible when friendship is dominated, not by a desire for temporal advantages, but by a *"love that is pure and unselfish."*[26] Characteristic of this unselfish love, and at the same time a proof of true friendship, is the willingness that is shown in bearing the burdens of a friend without complaining. For example, says Augustine:

You bear the burden of your brother's anger when you do not become angry with him. Then, on some other occasion, when you are disturbed by anger, let him put up with you peacefully and compassionately.[27]

While putting up with another's burdens is not an easy task, it is all too true that we do this more readily when these others are our friends, because we tend to make allowances or excuses for their weaknesses: *"Their good qualities appeal to us and support us."*[28]   Morever, this difficult task is inspired by our knowledge that the Lord Jesus willingly took upon himself our burdens and bore them in his suffering for love of us:

> Nothing could make us willingly take up such a weighty task
> as carrying the burdens of others, except it be the consideration of
> how much the Lord has suffered for us.[29]

Genuine love is the very core of friendship. It is this same love which keeps real friendship from becoming exclusive, or particular. It is precisely such love which also keeps us from cutting others off, as it demands openness toward all:

> No one seeking to unite himself with us in friendship is to be re-
> jected. It is not a question of accepting him immediately, but
> of wanting to accept him. Therefore, he should be treated in such a
> manner that this becomes possible.[30]

3. TRUST AND FRANKNESS ARE ESSENTIAL

The trust or confidence that exists between true friends is so great that it is often characterized by a sharing of their inmost thoughts. When we are willing to share in this fashion, we become aware of having accepted a person as a real friend.[31]   Moreover, such sharing means that we have come to see God in that person, and therefore we feel we are entrusting these thoughts not just *"to another human being, but to God in whom that person dwells."*[32]   This is really another manifestation of that deep love which is the foundation of all friendship.

But as trust brings about this sharing, it is frankness prompted by love which makes us speak up in order to help our friends know themselves better, correct themselves when necessary, and overcome difficulties with greater ease.[33]

> For the most part, enemies who call you to account are more useful than friends who are afraid to reproach you.[34]

And so Augustine goes on to say:

> No one can be truly a friend to another if he is not first of all a friend of the truth.... When I speak up for your good, I will be all the more frank with you the more I am your friend, because I will be all the more a friend the more I am faithful to you.[35]

But if friendship obliges one to speak up, it also obliges the other to be willing to accept the friend's efforts to help, painful though these may be at times. This is well illustrated in Augustine's life.

In a friendly manner, he once wrote to St. Jerome, whom he had never met. But he also criticized Jerome for some phrases of his translation of the Bible. Letter delivery was a haphazard process in those days, and letters were considered public domain, just like a postcard today. This particular letter of Augustine took ten years to reach Jerome, but before it got to him it had been read and copied along the way! In fact, it would seem that Jerome got one of the copies and wasn't even sure it was from Augustine. Jerome wrote a rather blistering letter in reply, which reached Augustine in just a few months. How Augustine replied to this severe correction by Jerome is admirable:

> I shall most gratefully receive a rebuke offered in such a friendly way.... If I receive your correction calmly as a medicine, I shall not be pained by it.... And even though because of a natural or personal

weakness I cannot help feeling saddened . . . it is better to put up with
the pain while the abscess on the head is being healed, rather than not
be cured so as to avoid the pain.[36]

Despite the fact that these two giants of the Church never met,
they had the highest esteem for one another, and their correspondence showed real love and friendship, despite occasional
misunderstandings.

Friends must believe in one another if they are to trust one
another. They must be willing to accept correction as well as
praise and appreciation. Such trust is as necessary between
friends as between parents and their children, teachers and their
pupils, husbands and wives, and in other human relationships.[37]

Much of what has been said so far refers particularly to the
traditional understanding of friendships as a close relationship.
However, in his great faith Augustine envisions friendship as
Jesus did, as embracing people on a much broader scale.

Friendship must not be circumscribed by narrow limits. It embraces
all those to whom affection and love are due, even though it goes
out more readily to some and turns more hesitantly toward others.
Friendship even extends to our enemies, for whom we are also
obliged to pray. Therefore, there is no one in the human race to
whom love is not owed, if not by reason of mutual affection, at least
because we share a common human nature. On the other hand, it is
only right that those especially delight us, by whom we are mutually
loved in a holy and chaste way.[38]

In this particular passage Augustine is evidently equating
friendship with fraternal charity. This is clear when we consider
that one of the prerequisites of true friendship is the return of
love that is offered. Such a return of love is certainly not present
when we are dealing with enemies. Yet here Augustine reveals
his very creative view of friendship. He would have us act always
with love, even regarding those who declare themselves our

enemies, and this with the hope and desire that they will change their attitudes and lay aside their enmity. In this way, we clearly will be loving and acting in the same manner that Jesus used toward us, seeing others not only for what or who they are at this moment in time, but for what or who they can become in the future through the grace of God.[39]

Living in Unity and Harmony Means Living as Friends

The ideas expressed above clearly concern all Christians. But now I would like to apply this in the context of religious or community life.

If friendship is so important for Augustine, we may well ask why he does not mention it in the *Rule* he wrote for religious. The answer would seem to lie in repeating what was said elsewhere concerning the word "community": "community" appears explicitly only once in the *Rule*; the word "friendship" is not even found there. Yet both concepts are basic to the *Rule*.[40]

Consider, for example, how Augustine emphasized that such a union of hearts existed between himself and his friends that they were no longer two but only one.[41] He repeats this idea in his *Commentary on Psalm 132*, which concerns the religious life. In it he defines what the Greek word "Monos" (= one) meant for him: not one alone, but *many becoming one.*[42] He mentions the same idea when he writes to Laetus, one of his religious who had left the community on a temporary basis. In this letter he speaks of the brothers in the monastery as being *"not many souls, but only one. . . ."*[43] And this is really the same thing he says at the beginning of the *Rule* when he charges his followers to live together in harmony and to be one in heart and soul as they tend toward God?[44]

The idea of friendship is at the very heart of the *Rule*, for those who are one in heart and soul are clearly friends, in God above all, but through God also in their love and care for one

another.[45]   Furthermore, true friendship is based on unselfish
love, and surely this is what Augustine is trying to say when he
urges religious to grow in love by putting the common interests
ahead of their own. He makes very clear that when religious seek
the common interest first, they are also really seeking their own
deepest interests, because they are committed to becoming one
community in Christ.

Applying Augustine's Views to Religious Life Today

The initial exhortations of the *Rule*, then, can be rightly
viewed as an appeal to live in friendship in the religious life. The
real proof of that friendship, however, will come only through
our willingness to bear one another's burdens. What are some of
these burdens? They could be illness, discouragement, misunderstandings; or as Augustine implies: anger, envy, impatience,
pride, and in other words, the very burden of sin itself, in our
lives and in that of our fellow religious.

But just how willing are we to put ourselves out to help our
friends and to bear their burdens with them? Friendship requires
frankness and truthfulness, but it also implies that we respect the
human nature of our friends, that when we seek to help them, we
do so with great gentleness and understanding; that we do not
hide the truth for fear of losing or breaking up our friendship.
Hiding the truth would not be a friendly act, but a very un-
friendly one. According to Augustine's view of things, as we
have already seen, there should be an unspoken rule among
those who live in community: they should want to be helped
mutually, not only through due affirmation, encouragement and
appreciation, but also through necessary fraternal correction,
accomplished with love. What a difference such an attitude
could make among religious everywhere!

These considerations can lead us to ask some very per-
tinent questions: Are we at least open to friendship with those

who share life with us, realizing, as Augustine urges, that we can never really know others except through friendship?[46]   Or are we only prepared to live together under the same roof physically and materially, without allowing an external harmony and unity to penetrate to the depths of our lives?[47]   Have we adopted a creative attitude in our love for others, a willingness, that is, to look beyond where a person is at present to where he or she might be through growth in the future? Moreover, given the fact that true friendship is a gift of God, which brings us closer not only to our friend but to Jesus himself, do we ever pray for the grace of friendship?

Casting Out Loneliness

One of the great banes of our society is the loneliness of so many of our fellow-citizens in this world. Mother Teresa of Calcutta has dedicated herself to helping the neediest of these lonely people. But perhaps all of us could contribute a little more to alleviating this unfortunate situation. How many times have we perhaps observed lonely religious, living right in the heart of our communities? We all need to be alone at times, but loneliness is quite another thing. It is one of the most painful experiences a person can undergo. It is to feel alone even though surrounded by others, to lack the courage to share with others what is happening deep within us: struggles, joys, frustrations. It is not to feel accepted.

On the other hand, how marvelous to have a trusty friend to listen to us, encourage us, and feel with us. We may well ask: How is it even possible that there be lonely people in the religious life, especially when Augustine has emphasized so clearly by word and example the necessity and the consolation of friendship?[48] I fear it is frequently because many have yearned for friendship at one time or another and have been badly burned in the process. As a result they have lost trust and have retreated into a shell to protect themselves from further disappointment and suffering. Perhaps they need to be encouraged to try again. Jesus too must have felt himself badly burned on occasion, even by those he considered friends. Yet he didn't give up: he kept giving love, even when it wasn't always returned. We should not be unwilling to run the risk of loving for fear it not be returned. On the other hand, if any of us have brought loneliness on ourselves by seeking our friends only or principally outside the community, isn't it time we also cultivated them at home?

There are many other questions that could be asked concerning friendship. But while we continue to question ourselves, perhaps we could also reflect on what more we could be doing to make this striking Christian characteristic more a part of our own lives and of those of our communities. Then we will be better able to understand and appreciate the joy and consolation of that friendship which Augustine so frequently speaks about and sums up so well in these words:

> I do confess that I cast myself without reservation on the love of those who are especially close to me, particularly when worn out by the upsets of the world. I rest in their love without the slightest worry, because I perceive that God is present there. . . . In this security I am undisturbed by fear of the uncertainty of the morrow. For when I see that a person is aflame with Christian love and has therefore become a faithful friend to me, I know that whatever thoughts or considerations I entrust to him, I entrust not to another human being, but to God in whom that person dwells, and by whom he is who he is.[49]

4

SEARCHING FOR GOD:
Contemplation and the Interior Life

PROBABLY THE MOST FAMOUS LINE that Augustine ever wrote is to be found in the opening paragraph of his equally famous book, The *Confessions: "You have made us for yourself, Lord, and our heart is restless until it rests in you."*[1]   That line may identify Augustine to all who know him, but what it says identifies the reality of all men and women: our basic human restlessness is due to the fact that we have not yet achieved the full purpose of our existence. And quite frankly, we can never fully achieve it here on earth. We are on pilgrimage, and our hearts are driven by a tremendous urge to find and possess that happiness which alone can satisfy us. In what he wrote, Augustine simply put his finger on the object of our desires. Whether all recognize this or not, we are on our way to God, and we cannot be completely happy or at peace until we have fully found him.

Searching for Love

The search for true happiness, for God himself, created a tremendous drive in Augustine as he was growing into manhood, though at the time, he himself, like so many young people today, may not have recognized this desire for happiness for what it really was:

> I sought for something to love, for I was in love with love. . . . For there was a hunger within me from a lack of inner food, which is you yourself, my God. Yet that hunger did not make me hungry. I had no desire for incorruptible food, not because I was already filled with it, but because the more I was empty of it, the more it was loathsome to me.[2]

Augustine wanted to love and be loved, but in a sensual way. He also wanted to take hold of the truth, make it his own and be filled with wisdom. He was searching for the basic answers to the mystery of life. In his own way, he was truly searching for God. Why he could not find him, he himself tells us:

> Where was I when I sought you? You were before me, but I had departed even from myself; I did not find myself, how much less you![3]

> You were within me, while I was outside: it was there that I sought you, and, a deformed creature, rushed headlong upon these things of beauty which you have made. You were with me, but I was not with you. They kept me far from you, those fair things which, if they were not in you, would not exist at all.[4]

The young Augustine had failed to grasp the very meaning of his existence, that is, the depth of the beauty which, deep within, was his as a result of the love of God at work in him through Christ Jesus. Like so many others of his time and ours, he traveled far and wide to marvel at the mountains, at the broad expanse of the oceans, at the rushing rivers weaving their way through hills and valleys, at the myriad patterns of the stars, but himself he passed by and neglected. He never stopped to look closely enough at himself, to try to understand himself better, to know who he really was.[5]

Searching with Determination

One thing, however, was very much in Augustine's favor: he always kept trying. No matter how discouraged, he never gave up. And this was really what saved him. With the coming of faith, he was finally able to perceive that God was indeed very close to him. God had been within him all along, even before Augustine discovered any personal relationship with him.[6] He even grew to the awareness that God was nearer to him than he was to himself.[7] Through his conversion Augustine became a great apostle of the interior life, because he came to realize that this was where Jesus the Christ was really to be found. His determination to find God at all costs is well expressed in this passage:

> I seek my God in the material things of heaven and earth, and I do not find him. I seek the reality of him in my own soul, and I do not find it. Yet I am determined to seek my God and, in my yearning to understand and look into the invisible things of God by means of created things, "I pour out my soul within me!" (Ps 42:5) I have no other purpose henceforth but to reach my God.[8]

The fact that Augustine remained convinced of the need to search for God by fostering a deep interior life, even while engaged in the diverse activities demanded of him by his apostolic life, offers encouragement to so many others who find themselves in similar circumstances today. That there is need for such encouragement is all too evident, because it is very easy to neglect the contemplative dimension of the consecrated life with the weak excuse that there is too much work to be done.

Augustine did not hesitate to speak frequently about the interior life, about contemplation, even to the laity. He also wrote on this subject whenever he had the chance.[9]   We may even say that his contemplative orientation dominates the pages of his *Confessions*, for this book is not only a confession of failings and sins, but perhaps especially a confession, or praise, of God.

What I would like to reflect on now is not intended to teach anyone an Augustinian method of interior prayer or contemplation. Quite truthfully, Augustine taught no such method. But maybe as we listen to him speaking about his own search for God and how he encouraged others to go about it, we will find it easier to be drawn to this type of prayer ourselves, or to persevere if we are already practicing it.

Turn Back Within

The depths of the interior life to which Augustine summons all Christians can be glimpsed in the following quotation:

> Do not go outside yourself, but turn back within; truth dwells in the inner man; and if you find your nature given to frequent change, go beyond yourself. . . . Move on, then, to that source where the light of reason itself receives its light.[10]

If there is one thing that Augustine emphasizes over and over again in treating of the search for God, it is that we must begin by going within ourselves. The key word is *within*. There we will find truth, light, joy, Christ himself. There we will be heard when we pray; there we will love and worship God. But while this *within* signifies the very depths of our being, this is only the first stage of our journey. Augustine urges us to keep moving on, even to what is beyond ourselves, to the very source of our inspiration and light, to God himself.

I sought the Lord, and he answered me" (Ps 34:5). Where did the
Lord hear? Within. Where does he give reply? Within. There you
pray, there you are heard, there you are made happy. . . . The one
standing near you knows nothing of this, for everything happens
in a hidden way, as the Lord indicates in the Gospel: 'Go to your
room, close your door, and pray to your Father in private. Then
your Father, who sees what no one sees, will repay you' (Mt 6:6).
Therefore, when you enter your room, you enter your heart. Happy
those who delight to enter their hearts and find no evil there.[11]

Augustine uses various words to designate where, within
ourselves, we are to find the Lord: in our heart, our conscience,
our hidden places, our inner chamber, our inner being. But all
these mean the same thing: the very depths of our being, where
God dwells and waits for us. Furthermore, it seems Augustine
can never emphasize sufficiently the great joy and happiness
which such interior communication with God actually brings
with it. He gently chides his faithful for erroneously thinking
that the things of the Lord, such as meditation, discovering the
Creator in nature, worshiping and loving God, cannot bring as
much joy as they find, say in fishing or hunting or the theater.

But let us also raise our affections beyond ourselves and not limit
ourselves to joy in temporal things. We too have a chamber. Why do
we not enter into it? . . . Why do we not reflect upon the everlasting
years and find joy in the works of the Lord? . . . Who can live without joy? Do you think, brothers and sisters, that those who reverence
and worship and love God have no joys? Do you really think that
the arts and the theater, and hunting and fowling and fishing, all
bring joy, but God's works do not? Do you think that meditation on
God does not bring its inner joys, when a man looks upon the
universe and the spectacle of nature and seeks out its maker and finds
a creator who is never displeasing but supremely pleasing?[12]

Jesus, the Way and the Goal

At the same time that we are invited to enter into ourselves to find God, we are reminded forcefully that the only one who can lead us fruitfully to this goal is Christ Jesus himself, the Son of God.[13]   As Augustine puts it, Christ is both the way and the goal.

> Through the man Christ you go to the God Christ. God means much to you, but God became man. The Word which was far from you became man in your midst. Where you are to abide, he is God; on your way there, he is man. Christ himself is both the Way by which you go and the Haven toward which you make your way.[14]

Time and again Augustine underlines the fact that through faith Christ is already within us, that he alone is the interior Master, and that all of us must learn from him. The preacher's word may fall on our ears, but unless we have Christ within and are willing to listen to him, we will not understand what God is trying to tell us through his minister.

> We have our teacher within, Christ. If you cannot grasp something through your ear and my mouth, turn to him in your hearts, for it is he who teaches me what to say and gives to you as he wishes.[15]

> Unless there is one who teaches within, the sound we make is futile. . . . Let him then speak to you interiorly, in that place where no human teacher can enter.[16]

> "Enter", then, "into your heart" (Is 46:8), and if you have faith, you will find Christ there. There he speaks to you. I, the preacher, must raise my voice, but he instructs you more effectively in silence.[17]

The Search Makes Demands

Because Jesus instructs interiorly in silence, we must foster within ourselves an atmosphere of silence. While it is a great help to be able to get away from the noise and confusion of the world around us, this is not always possible for many people. What we must do, however, is know how to free ourselves from these disturbances within, in our hearts, so that we will have a chance to listen to Christ and not just to ourselves with all our pains and feelings and built-in prejudices.

> Let us leave a little room for reflection, room too for silence. Enter into yourself, leave behind all noise and confusion. Look within yourself and see whether there be some delightful hidden place in your consciousness where you can be free of noise and argument, where you need not be carrying on your disputes and planning to have your own stubborn way. Hear the word in quietness, that you may understand it.[18]

But if all this is necessary in the ordinary course of events in order to understand Christ, our interior Master, much more will we need an atmosphere of attentive inner silence when we seek to go deeper into ourselves along the ways of interior prayer or contemplation. Furthermore, we will need to nourish ourselves, as Augustine did, with frequent, prolonged reading and reflection on the Scriptures. Such reading will lead us both to listen and to dialogue with the Master. We must also purify the eye of the heart so that we will be able to see God,[19]   and be willing to give up every other love but that of God. Such a purification is painful, but it is a necessary prelude to becoming more sensitive to the presence of God within.

> A person would desire, if it were possible, to obtain at once the joys of lovely and perfect wisdom, without the endurance of toil in action and suffering, but that is impossible in this mortal life. . . . So in the discipline of man, the toil of doing the work of righteousness precedes the delight of understanding the truth.[20]

Fraternal Love Leads to God

Father Athanasius Sage, an Assumptionist priest who, during his lifetime wrote many excellent works on St. Augustine, once commented that Augustine insisted on fraternal charity as the best way of flying toward contemplation. And this, he added, only serves to emphasize the originality of Augustine's teaching.[21]   This indication fits in very well with what we know of Augustine's broader ideas about the Christian life, namely, that we are to honor and serve God in our brothers and sisters by the love and concern we show them and by bearing their burdens with them.[22]   Augustine even goes so far as to say that it is by loving our brothers and sisters that we come to see God, that we love love itself:

> If you love your brother whom you see, by that very fact you will also see God, because you will see charity itself and God dwells in the interior.[23]

What is even more important is that this love of our neighbor is the way in which we purify our interior vision so we can see God:

> You, however, who do not yet see God, by loving your neighbor will make yourself worthy of seeing him. By loving your neighbor you cleanse your eyes so you can see God. . . . Love your neighbor, then, and see within yourself the source of this love of neighbor; there you will see God insofar as you are able.[24]

Furthermore, if we want to recognize Christ here on earth, we are urged to act towards others as the disciples of Emmaus acted toward the unknown pilgrim who joined them along the way: *"They received him with gracious courtesy,"* says Augustine. *". . . Hospitality restored what unbelief had taken away."*[25]

It is very important to remember that, for Augustine, love of neighbor is not something theoretical. This love makes very practical demands on all, or it is not real love at all. For example, among those who are striving to live in community, it demands a daily effort to achieve real unity and harmony, to overcome the very human problems which can constantly arise and impede progress. In other words, it demands that we bear one another's burdens. This is the way to love and fulfill the law of Christ! In Augustine's mind fraternal harmony has a real social dimension. The fact that harmony and unity are sought and lived in a given community shows that Christ is really present there. This is the chief way by which religious purify themselves interiorly so that they can more easily see and recognize Christ.[26]

Searching and Sharing

Augustinian-oriented contemplation also demands that we put ourselves at the service of others through the apostolate. No one should be so given to contemplation, Augustine remarks, that they give no thought to their neighbor's needs.[27] In other words, as he sees it, not even the purely contemplative life is free of apostolic responsibility. The search for the truth in itself requires intense activity, but the truth which may be discerned is not to be considered a private possession. It is to be shared with others. This responsibility may weigh especially on those who have real talents for teaching or writing or counseling, even among those who live a strictly contemplative life.[28] However, probably the most compelling proof of the need for all to show love to their neighbor lies in Jesus' description of the last judgment.[29] As Jesus points out, no great feats are demanded of anyone. But all without exception will be judged by their concern (or lack of it!) for God's little ones, the needy. Therefore, Augustine tells us: "*When you have found your way back to*

*yourself, don't stay locked up within yourself. . . . Turn to the one who
made you.*"[30]

> The Lord cries out to us to come and drink, if we thirst interiorly.
> Moreover, he says that if we drink, rivers of living water will flow
> from our depths. The depths of the interior person is the conscience
> of his heart. By drinking this liquid, the cleansed conscience comes to
> life again, and disposes of a fountain, from which it can drink. *What
> is this fountain,* and what is this river that flows forth from the depths
> of the interior person. *The benevolence which leads him to be concerned
> for his neighbor.* For if he were to think that what he drinks in is only
> for himself, there would be no living waters flowing from his depths.
> But if he hastens to care for his neighbor, the water will not dry up; it
> will keep right on flowing.[31]

If we really desire to enter into contemplation with the
Lord and drink at his interior fount, we must be prepared to
share this great gift with others. As Augustine wrote: "*(My) heart
burns, but not for myself alone; it desires to be at the service of
fraternal love.*"[32]

Augustine also firmly believed that it would be easier to
come to know and love God in a community of friends, where
each would share with the others any graces or lights received.
This early desire, expressed shortly after his conversion, was
translated into reality only two years later with the founding of
his first religious community in Tagaste. Augustine once asked
himself why he wanted his friends to live with him on a perma-
nent basis, and this is how he replied:

> So that we may search for the knowledge of God and of the soul in
> fraternal harmony. In this way the one who first arrives at the truth
> can communicate it easily to the others. . . . They will be so much
> the more friends for me insofar as our Beloved is more fully shared by
> all of us.[33]

The search for God through contemplation, or interior
prayer, is not, therefore, an inner process which affects only one

person. Because it is a process characterized by growing love, it is made to be shared with others and to radiate joy to them. Furthermore, it is an ongoing task. Growth in this kind of prayer is likened to passing from the stages of infancy, where much milk is necessary, to that of maturity, where grown persons are nourished by solid food, which itself is ever better assimilated with the passing of time. But the growth is clearly from God who gives those seeking him more and more light as they strive to draw closer to him.

> Therefore, in the mind itself, that is, in the interior person, growth takes place in such a way that, not only does one pass from milk to solid food, but this solid food itself is assimilated in ever greater proportions. This growth is not something physical, but consists in a clearer interior light, because the food itself is intelligible light. Therefore, if you would grow and understand God . . . then you must seek and hope, not from that teacher who knocks at your ears . . . but from him who gives the growth.[34]

The Search Is Never Over

Since God never forces himself on anyone, but rather attracts us to himself through the delight of what he is and what he teaches,[35] at times interior prayer may even bring with it some special light or consolation. But such are normally short-lived. They do not constitute the purpose of contemplative prayer or of communioning with God. Augustine has some remarkable passages which certainly express his own experience in this regard. But even in the midst of being lifted up, as it were, he manages to keep his feet quite firmly on the ground:

> The one who walks in this tent, and turns over in his mind the wonderful things God has done for the redemption of the faithful is struck and bewitched by the sounds of that festival in heaven, drawn by them like the stag to the fountain of waters. But as long as we are in the body, my brothers and sisters, we are traveling abroad from

God and the corruptible body weighs down the soul, and this earthly
dwelling presses on the mind that thinks many things. And so even
if, by walking in desire, we manage somehow or other to dispel the
clouds and to reach up to those sounds at times . . . yet under the
burden of our weakness we fall back again to the humdrum things
we are used to. And just as up there we found something to rejoice
about, so here there is no lack of something to groan about.[36]

Some of Augustine's most challenging thoughts regarding
interior prayer can be seen in the way he urges us to keep moving
forward, to continue searching and finding, because the search is
never fully over till we have reached the goal of our lives. Even in
heaven the search will continue, in the sense that we shall
constantly discover more and more of the boundlessness of God.
What Augustine is pointing out in all this is the fact that we must
never allow ourselves to grow satisfied with what we may have
already achieved. God is never fully possessed in this life. He is
always drawing us on to something deeper, if we know how to
heed his call.

Let us seek him out in order to find him, and when we find him, let us
continue searching for him. We must search for him, because he is
hidden from us. And when we have found him, we go on searching
because he is without bounds. . . . He fills the one who seeks him,
insofar as his capacity permits; and he increases that capacity in the
one who finds him, so that he might again seek to be filled.[37]

We search for God in order to find him with greater joy, and we find
him in order to keep searching with greater love.[38]

The Apostolate of the Contemplative

I would like to consider briefly something I left suspended
above concerning the specific apostolate of those who live a
strictly contemplative life in the Church, for these men and
women are not always fully appreciated, even by good Catholics.

When Augustine wrote to the monks of Capraria — who appear to have been living a strictly contemplative life — he did not tell them to go outside their monastery to get involved in an active apostolate, except in the case that the Church would request this of them. But he did tell them that they had a real apostolate to carry out right there in the monastery, and primarily among themselves. He emphasized their need to work, but all this work was well within the ambient of their contemplative life. For example, he told them to work solely for the glory of God, and to work enthusiastically at praying, fasting and above all at fraternal love. While this love should also embrace the needy outside the monastery, it was equally addressed to fostering forgiveness within the community and with bearing one another's burdens willingly. They were to work at subjecting their bodies and at discerning good and evil spirits. They were to work at praising the Lord in the Liturgy of the Hours. In brief, their main work was directed toward their sanctification and toward sharing with others the Christian values they discovered.[39]

If we were to sum up the "activities" which were expected of those monks, we would rightly say that their great task was to be transformed into Christ and to share the presence of Christ with all around them. But contemplatives can do even more for those outside the monastery or convent. By their very lives they are a sign of protest to many of the false values which are proposed by society. They teach others, therefore, the true values of life, that real joy does not consist in owning many things, but in humbly recognizing that we belong to God.

They teach us how to appreciate and find true peace, interior peace, that peace which can only come from the presence of God in the soul. They give concrete meaning to the communion of saints, even here on earth, for they lighten the burden of those who are spiritually weaker. They literally bear in themselves many of the sufferings and crosses which might otherwise be ours and which could easily overwhelm us, and they teach us the spirit in which we should bear the crosses which do come to us. They also teach us the tremendous power of prayer, faith and love in a world that seems to believe only in the power of money, weapons, and violence. Their loving presence in the Church, their concern for all men and women as they are in the sight of God, their deep desire to praise God and render Christ present in our times constitute spiritual works of mercy which are of incalculable aid to all God's little ones. They, more than others, generously fulfill the admonition of Jesus concerning the last judgment, even though they are not specifically aware of whom they may have served in this fashion.

Summing Up

If we go back and reflect on Augustine's way to God and his search for God through a deeply interior life, several things seem to stand out.

First of all, though surrounded by noise, confusion, anxieties and the many problems of his pastoral service, Augustine never failed to create within himself, through faith and grace, an interior silence which allowed him to commune with God the Father and his Son Jesus. His total focus was on Jesus Christ, both as the one who would lead him within, and as the one who was the goal of his interior search. Furthermore, he nourished himself thoroughly on the Scriptures, reading, reflecting and sharing with others what lights he may have received. He knew the need to purify the eye of the heart, if he was to see God and recognize him. He well understood that the fatigue of working toward love had to precede the joy of grasping the truth, which is God himself. That is why he concentrated so heavily on working for unity and harmony in the community, on loving his fellow men and women, especially those nearest to him and on bearing their burdens with them. Augustine was convinced that this was the quickest and surest way of achieving interior peace and of creating an environment which would enable one to search for and find God. He allowed the universe and all God's marvelous creation to lead him to the Creator, but he knew that he would find his Maker only within, in the depths of his own heart. He did not allow himself to be discouraged when his interior prayer was rudely interrupted and he was forced back to the humdrum realities of life. He knew that his search had to continue, and that it would never be totally completed because of the hiddenness and boundlessness of God.

The only conclusion I wish to draw from all this is that contemplation is not out of the reach of ordinary mortals such as ourselves. Moreover, for those who have been in the religious or priestly life for a number of years, the interior prayer which Augustine speaks of should be a natural stage of growth in simplifying prayer life. Interior silence, knowledge of the Scriptures, and an ongoing purification are prerequisites to this prayer. Love of neighbor, carried to the point of self-forgetfulness, will open inner eyes to God's presence in ourselves, as well as in others. And Jesus himself is the guide to whom we entrust ourselves in our search for the Father.

The author of *The Cloud of Unknowing* sums up quite well the paradox of contemplation:

> If you ask me just precisely how one is to go about doing the contemplative work of love, I am at a complete loss. All I can say is I pray that Almighty God in his great goodness and kindness will teach you himself. For in all honesty I must admit I do not know. And no wonder, for it is a divine activity and God will do it in whomever he chooses. . . . I assure you, contemplation is not the fruit of study, but a gift of grace.[40]

What this gift of grace did for Augustine, what it meant to him, and how it affected his whole being, and all his senses, can be very well summed up in his own words, which provide a fitting conclusion for these reflections:

> You have called to me, and have cried out, and have shattered my
> deafness.
> You have blazed forth with light, and have shone upon me, and you
> have put my blindness to flight!
> You have sent forth fragrance, and I have drawn in my breath, and I
> pant after you.
> I have tasted you, and I hunger and thirst after you.
> You have touched me, and I have burned for your peace.[41]

5

SIGN OF CONTRADICTION

A FEW YEARS AGO I was in the Philippines, giving a talk on Augustine to the professors and some 300 students of the Augustinian University of San Agustin in the southern city of Iloilo. At one point I made them aware of that "strange prayer" which Augustine in his youth had once addressed to the Father, a prayer which, I said, had probably been repeated by young people of all generations from time immemorial:

> I . . . had even sought chastity from you [Lord] and had said, 'Give me chastity and continence, but not yet!' For I feared that you would hear me quickly, and that quickly you would heal me of that disease of lust which I wished to have satisfied rather than extinguished.[1]

I had no sooner concluded this quotation when there were almost audible gasps from among the students as its meaning sank in: complete identification had been established between the man who wrote those lines in the 4th century and these young people of the 20th century with their own particular problems. So true was this that at the end of the talk, during a question and answer period, I was asked by one of the young ladies present if Augustine had any more things to say like that!

A Conflict of the Heart

As a matter of fact, Augustine has a lot to say about things "like that": about virginity, chastity and continence; about the tremendous conflict that took place in his own heart and mind as he struggled to shake off the iron bonds of sensual desire that held him fast and to replace them with the freedom that comes with a chaste service of the Lord.

> The enemy had control of my will, and out of it he fashioned a chain and fettered me with it. . . . A new will which had begun within me, to wish freely to worship you and find joy in you, O God . . . was not yet able to overcome that prior will, grown strong with age. Thus did my two wills, the one old, the other new, the first carnal, and the second spiritual, contend with one another, and by their conflict they laid waste my soul.[2]

In his total honesty Augustine does not spare himself the pain of recounting scenes which show the depths to which he had descended before he found his way to Jesus Christ. At the same time, however, he brings out clearly the joy and happiness that were his once he began to live a holy and chaste life in the Lord.

Augustine's problems began early in his homelife. As he tells us, his father, who at the time was still a pagan, was much more interested in his son's coming career and in his cultivated speech, than in how chaste he was or in how he was growing in the sight of God.[3]   (By way of parentheses we could well ask ourselves if things are much different today, even in some homes that call themselves Christian.) Interior confusion swept over

Augustine in his years of puberty, as it does over all youth, *"So that I could not distinguish the calm light of chaste love from the fog of lust."*[4]   Until his conversion at thirty-two years of age, he experienced a tremendous pull towards sinful sexual activity. Later, as a bishop, and undoutedly drawing on his personal experience, he would counsel the neophytes whom he was about to baptize that, *"In holy baptism your sins will be forgiven, but your passions will remain; against these, then, you will have to fight even after you are reborn."*[5]   On one occasion, while preaching to his people, he remarked: *"The concupiscence with which we are born will never die out as long as we live; it may grow daily weaker, but it will never die out."*[6]   And while he thanked God for the great gift of continence which had been given him with the faith, he confessed openly that he was still assailed by the images that former sinful habits had implanted in his memory:

> In truth, you command me to be continent. . . . You have commanded me to abstain from concubinage, and in place of marriage itself, which you permit, you have counseled something better. Since you granted this to me, it has been fulfilled even before I became a dispenser of your sacrament. Yet in my memory, of which I have said mamy things, there still live images of such things as my former habits implanted there.[7]

It seems to me that this is where religious and priests today can best identify with that man of sixteen centuries ago, who was both religious and priest. God has counseled "something better" for us just as he did for Augustine, something that makes us gladly forego marriage. This "something better" has been our goal since entering the consecrated or priestly life. We have certainly striven to fulfill our solemn commitment to God, but like Augustine, we have also been subject to many and varied temptations. Perhaps we have even experienced some falls, not only because of memories that have welled up from the past, but also because of our very human nature and a daily encounter with the culture which surrounds us and even works its way into religious houses in the form of magazines, books and television programs. All around us we are confronted with a mentality which exalts sexual freedom, even the so-called need for genital activity, in order to achieve true human fulfillment.

The chastity, therefore, which we have joyfully taken upon ourselves for the sake of the kingdom, demands a determined effort. As any object of beauty and great value, it cannot be possessed unless we are willing to pay a proportionate price for it. And the price in this case is sincere prayer, humility by which we come to know our weaknesses, self-discipline and self-sacrifice. A vow of chastity has always demanded the best efforts of those who took it. Today, however, it is even more demanding because it is so evidently "counter-culture." Living such a life has even been described at times as *hazardous, harmful,* or *impossible.*[8]   But it is also a *sign of contradiction.* It makes people of good will ask themselves hard questions about what public witness means and why it is important, even necessary, in the total life of the Church.[9]   In an age of unrestrained indulgence and rampant materialism this sign of total commitment to God and to the service of his people is more necessary than ever.

Augustine's Views on Chastity in the Light of Faith

Augustine considered two things essential for those who wished to live the religious life with him: the vow or profession of the common life and a vow of chastity. Religious poverty and obedience were so incorporated into the reality of Augustine's ideal that they were an integral part of the vow of common life and not easily separated from it.[10]   Augustine's esteem for virginity, as well as for chastity in all walks of life, may be seen in the following passage, which is part of a sermon addressed to his people, treating first of the baptismal vows common to all Christians and then of individual vows:

Do not make vows and then neglect to keep them. . . . What vow are
we all expected to make without distinction? The vow of believing
in Christ, hoping for eternal life from him and living a good life
in keeping with the ordinary norms of good conduct. . . . But there
are also vows made by individuals: one vows to God conjugal
chastity. . . . Others, after having experienced the pleasures of
matrimony, vow to give up this union for the future. These vow
something greater than the former. Others make a vow of virginity
from their earliest years and give up completely those pleasures
which others abandon only after having tasted them. These make the
greatest vow of all. . . . Another makes a vow to give up all his goods
so that they may be distributed to the poor, and to live in community
in the company of the saints: this is a great vow. . . . Let each
one make the vow he wishes, but let him also take care to observe the
vow he has made."[11]

Religious chastity is really the most fundamental of all the
vows of religious life. During the course of the centuries the
manner of living the common life, as well as the manner of
practicing poverty and obedience, have varied in keeping with
the particular aims of different religious institutes. But though
there have been new insights into the affectivity of the human
person in our own days, there has been no essential change in
what is expected of a person consecrated to God by a vow of
chastity. Among all the evangelical counsels, this one, in the
words of the Second Vatican Council, stands out as a *surpassing
gift of grace.*"[12]

This is not, however, to ignore the special problems that
have arisen in our own times concerning intimacy, affection and
better integration of one's sexuality into community life. The
Council itself seems to take note of these needs when it says that,
*"chastity has stronger safeguards in a community when true frater-
nal love thrives among its members."*[13]   Really, all that is being
said in this book concerning community life and the need to love
one another, or concerning the sharing of one another's burdens,
encouraging one another and appreciating different needs — all

of this is also concerned in a general way with addressing this
particular point. Since the Council some progress has been made
in this area of the religious life. But frequently there is still a real
need to work better toward establishing the bases for a more
genuine rapport among the members of many of our communities. The solution to problems which arise in these areas is
not going to come from seeking to satisfy the real needs for
chaste intimacy, affection and integration by turning outside the
community to an environment that quite frankly often does not
even understand a vow of chastity. These real affective needs
should be able to be met and channeled in a healthy and chaste
way, beginning within our own communities, without giving in
to exaggerations or having unreal expectations of what the
community can provide.[14]

But if there is no question as to what is expected of a person
consecrated to God by chastity, there is likewise no question as
to the fact that people will not be able to live this vow by their
own efforts alone. Jesus himself made that clear when speaking
to his disciples: *"Not everyone can accept this teaching* [that it is
better not to marry]; *only those to whom it is given to do
so."*[15]   Yet Augustine tells us that in his early years he had been
foolish enough to believe *"that continence lay within a man's own
powers,"* not realizing *"that no one can be continent unless you
[Lord] grant it to him."*[16]   Indeed, *"Who is the man who will
reflect on his weakness, and yet dare to credit his chastity and
innocence to his own powers. . . ?"*[17]   And as we have seen,
Augustine as much as admitted that he had not really tried to be
chaste or even asked seriously for this grace because he feared
God would hear and heal him. And deep down that was not yet
what he wanted.[18]

Physically virginity is hallowed in the religious vow of
chastity. But this self-offering has no meaning whatsoever if it is
not accompanied by chastity of the spirit: *"No one,"* says
Augustine, *"preserves bodily purity unless chastity is already rooted*

in the spirit,"[19] which in its turn is grounded in *"an integral faith, a solid hope and a sincere love."*[20] What is truly important in the vow of chastity is not the fact that one foregoes marriage, or is more easily freed from a certain slavery to the attractions of the flesh. Rather, it is the fact that a person is totally consecrated to God, and as such made capable of loving God's people in a broader, more universal manner:

> We do not praise in virgins the fact that they are virgins, but the fact that they are consecrated to God by holy chastity.[21]

That Augustine emphasizes the interior more than the exterior aspects of chastity is brought out in the remarkable way in which he speaks of Mary, the Mother of God.

> It was for Mary a greater thing to have been Christ's disciple than to have been his mother. . . . It was a greater thing to keep God's truth in her heart, than to carry his flesh in her womb.[22]

In other words:

> Mary was more blessed in accepting the faith of Christ than in conceiving the flesh of Christ. . . . Even Mary's maternal relationship would have been of no advantage to her if she had not borne Christ more happily in her heart than in her flesh.[23]

Consecrated Chastity Must Lead to Love

Religious chastity is not just a question of giving up something! Like all the evangelical counsels, it must lead to love.[24] It is also true that religious chastity gives entry to the closest possible friendship with God. But since this friendship is founded on the observance of God's commandments of love, it must also reach out to the entire Church and to all people, or it will fail.[25] In brief, a vow of chastity constitutes a commitment not only to God, but also to the Church and to her pastoral ministry. It must lead us to become more loving and caring persons, not turn us in on ourselves in an egotistical manner. Chastity, therefore, cannot be limited to an intense love of God. It also embraces love of God's sons and daughters.[26] Moreover, this vow should better enable us to keep our priorities straight and make us less likely to be divided in our allegiances, because it directs the entire thrust of our lives toward pleasing God and following the lead of his Son through holiness in body and in spirit.[27]   Augustine emphasizes this unifying aspect of chastity and its outreach in these reflections:

> Continence brings us together and leads us back to that unity from which we have strayed toward a multitude of things. A person loves you less [O Lord] if he loves along with you something else which he does not love for your sake. O Love, ever burning, never extinguished, O Charity, my God, set me on fire![28]

> You have commanded upon us not only continence, that is, to withhold our love from certain things, but also justice, that is, whereon we are to bestow our love. You have willed not only that you yourself be loved by us, but our neighbor also.[29]

Augustine asked to be "set on fire" by God's love and to be outgoing in the manifestation of this love, for he well understood that *"a greater love has imposed a greater burden"* on those who are consecrated to God by chastity.[30]   But it is this same love which is the safeguard of one's consecrated chastity. The more we love as God has loved us, the more God will guard in us his own great and surpassing gift: our chastity.

> It is God alone, therefore, who both gives virginity and protects it. And God is love! Love, therefore, is the guardian of virginity, but humility is the dwelling-place of this guardian. He indeed dwells there who said that the Holy Spirit rests on the humble, the peaceful, and the one who fears his words. . . . Humble spouses more easily follow the Lamb than proud virgins.[31]

Living at Ease with the Vow of Chastity

Beautiful though the ideal may be, those attempting to live it know how much of a struggle is involved in striving for it. Augustine knew this struggle also: *"Do not be afraid of any external enemy,"* he said. *"Conquer yourself, and the world will have been overcome."*[32] But that is exactly where the difficulty lies, in conquering ourselves. There are effectively two wills and two loves fighting for supremacy in each of us: the love of the world and the love of God. These loves often manifest themselves in contrary affections and desires.[33] We are consecrated to God, but still subject to temptation. And because we know our weaknesses, we can all too easily fear the power of some of these temptations. Yet it is precisely when we find ourselves the weakest, that we can experience the great strength of God working in us and can truly prove our love for him:

> I willingly boast of my weaknesses that the power of Christ may rest upon me. Therefore, I am content with weakness, with mistreatment, with distress, with persecutions and difficulties for the sake of Christ, for when I am powerless, it is then that I am strong.[34]

I wonder what Augustine would have to say to us in a practical vein if he were speaking to us personally right now. Perhaps his whole approach would be summed up in those striking words of his, already cited: *"My God, set me on fire."*[35]

This is where I think Augustine would want us to begin, asking the Lord to set us on fire: with his love, his generosity, his self-sacrificing service and concern for others. Our vow of chastity must be centered in our hearts, more than in our minds. It must be founded on faith, hope and love, much more than on intellectual persuasion. Intellectual justification will never really satisfy us in this regard. Either the heart will be involved in this consecration — and deeply involved! — or chastity becomes impossible. Moreover, difficulties must be met with deep faith and love, as well as with the strength which God himself gives us.

And what is this strength which God gives us? Is it only that burst of interior grace which may save us, as it were, in the "nick of time"? Or is it grace, often wearing a very human form, which God puts in our path and asks us to accept in all simplicity and humility, without expecting miracles? Augustine believes in both kinds of graces, but his *Rule* in particular spells out several of these more human helps in a very practical way. Again, I think that if Augustine were with us today he would say: *Look around you! See what God is offering you here and now and make good use of it!*

What is it that God is offering us here and now? Above all a call to community, which, in the Augustinian sense of the term, is a call to love, to friendship, to sharing and to mutual concern. Our communities, therefore, cannot be just nice places to pray, work, eat and sleep. They are at the same time home, hearth and strength, because our communities are ourselves, you and me and all those who live with us.

Augustine's *Rule* is powerful in spelling out this strength in very concrete fashion. By mutual vigilance over one another,[36] by fraternal correction undertaken in the spirit of love,[37]   by concerned presence to one another even outside the walls of the religious house,[38]   religious offer a unique service of love which is vitally important in helping to live out one's consecration in chastity. A lived friendship with one another, which implies . truthfulness, frankness and trust, is also a constant source of encouragement. Furthermore, the spirit of prayer and of penance,[39]   which forms an integral part of community life, should remind us continually of the presence of God and of that salutary fear of God which is a source of strength and protection that we must not neglect.[40] Augustine gives even more practical hints in urging that religious not attract undue attention to themselves or give offense by what they wear, or by their walk, behavior or other activity.[41]   In other words, he appeals to simplicity of lifestyle as another real safeguard. But perhaps his most important advice in this matter is that religious forestall unnecessary difficulties by knowing and recognizing their weaknesses, that is, by being humble enough to exercise necessary checks on themselves, especially on their hearts.[42]   In all of this it is more than evident that Augustine is not asking us to expect miracles in order to be able to persevere in our consecration to God. Rather, he is insisting that God will be working principally in us through other good people and through the simple, ordinary things of everyday life.

Pride Goes Before the Fall

The old saying that pride goes before the fall was never any truer than in the case of safeguarding religious chastity: *"Let anyone who thinks he is standing firm, watch out lest he fall."*[43]   Religious who think that they can do anything, see anything, hear anything, or read anything just as though they had never taken a vow of chastity or consecrated themselves to God seem to be blissfully unaware of their very wounded human nature. They seem to be all too much like the proud Pharisee in the gospel who claimed he was "not like the rest of men," and certainly not like that humble tax-collector in the back of the synagogue, who admitted his weaknesses with bowed head.[44] No wonder Augustine has such reservations about someone professsing perpetual continence who may be free of many other vices and faults, but weighed down by pride. In the following quotes he is addressing himself to consecrated virgins, but what he says is applicable to all religious.

For her I fear pride; I am apprehensive of her becoming puffed up owing to so great a blessing. The more reason she finds in herself to be conceited, the more I fear that by pleasing herself she will displease him who "resists the proud, but gives grace to the humble."[45]

Therefore, let her first thought be to put on humility, lest she think that she is a virgin of God by her own doing, rather than that this finest gift comes down from above, from the Father.[46]

A Call to Generosity

By way of some concluding remarks, I would like to go back to something said previously concerning Augustine's attitude before his conversion, namely, that he as much as admitted that he had not really tried to be chaste and had not asked seriously for this grace. Sometimes a lot of difficulties with chastity stem, not from the fact that we do not really want to be chaste — we most certainly do! Rather, they stem from the fact that we are not always willing to expend the energy necessary in order to be generous in living this vow. And perhaps this is where we can hurt ourselves the most. For in matters of religious chastity, we only kid ourselves if we think we can exclude generosity from our commitment and rather try to live on some artificial borderline between what is permitted and what is not. The living of chastity for the sake of the kingdom can scarcely be realized by those who want to perform a kind of balancing act on a tightrope, very high in the air. The dizzy heights can make for a nasty fall. We have to learn to keep our feet firmly on the ground, recognize our human nature for what it is, and make the best use of God's helps, both spiritual and human. This is the way to remain faithful to our commitment.

No one can live a vow of chastity without a spirit of self-discipline and self-sacrifice. No one can expect to persevere in this holy commitment without seriously asking for help through prayer and by making frequent use of the sacramental helps the Church offers. Asceticism may not be a very popular word for many today, but what it represents is essential for the lives of those consecrated to God. There is no way the grain of wheat can bear fruit, unless it dies.[47]   There is no way religious can bear fruit in love, unless they die to themselves. God has extended a special invitation to us to take on, as Augustine puts it, *"something better"*, or as Paul says, *"to be holy and blameless . . . and filled with love."*[48]   Our heavenly Father also encourages us with words similar to those addressed to Mary at the Annunciation: "Do not be afraid! I am with you. Nothing is impossible with God."[49]   Yet, as we have seen, very much depends on us also. We must accept God's coming into our lives in a very personal way, trust him, and cooperate with the strength he offers us. Then we will know what it means to be set on fire with his love, and we will know also the tremendous joy of sharing with others the fullness of that love.

The following words of exhortation, addressed by Augustine to women consecrated to God, apply equally to consecrated Christians today and form a fitting conclusion to these thoughts on evangelical chastity:

> Let those among you who persevere be an example to you,
>   but let those who fall increase your fear.
> Hold dear the example of those who persevere and imitate it;
>   weep for those who fall, lest you grow proud.
> Do not proclaim your own righteousness;
>   submit yourself to God who frees you from blame.
> Pardon the sins of others; pray for your own.
> Avoid future falls by your vigilance;
>   blot out those of the past by confession.[50]

CHAPTER **6**

THE COMMITTED CHRISTIAN AND THE CROSS

THE SECOND VATICAN COUNCIL launched a challenge to all Christians to make them better appreciate their role in the Church and live it to the fullest extent of their ability. All baptized persons, for example, were reminded of their call to holiness, an area that for all too long had been considered the exclusive domain of priests and religious.[1]   The entire Church was made more keenly aware of its fundamental missionary nature and of the practical consequences which follow from this.[2]   The laity were urged to take their rightful, active part in the apostolate, in keeping with their own particular role in society, and to be no longer merely passive spectators in their Church.[3]   And while it was emphasized to religious that their one supreme law and fundamental norm was none other than the *following of Christ as proposed by the Gospel,*[4]   they were also challenged to *"consider carefully that through them, to believers and non-believers alike, the Church truly [wishes] to give an increasingly clearer revelation of Christ."*[5] In other words, religious were reminded forcefully that their vocation was to be radical Christians, totally committed to God's service and to the imitation of Jesus in such a way that their lives would more clearly reflect Christ's life in the world today.

To be a radical Christian in this sense is no easy task. It demands that a person literally want to "put on Christ," be Christ for others, with the same gentleness and mercy that Jesus showed during his earthly life. This of course means that such persons are willing to love as Christ did, strip themselves of all that could get in the way of communicating him and his message to others, and be prepared to sacrifice, not others, but themselves, for the spreading of his kingdom.[6]

Becoming more like Christ, however, is not something that happens suddenly, or once and for all. Like any conversion it is an ongoing process, which requires concerned cooperation and a willingness to struggle all during life. Human nature does not yield easily to the growth of a selfless love such as Jesus modeled in his life. There are strong egotistical tendencies and instincts to be overcome, as well as that fundamental craving of the flesh, the eyes and worldly ambition which exert such a strong pull on our whole being. Drawing on his own wealth of experience in this regard, Augustine commented in one of his sermons:

> As long as we live here on earth, my brothers and sisters, this is the way it will be. We have grown old in this combat and now encounter weaker foes, but they are still foes. Age has even somewhat worn them out, but they do not yet cease to disturb the peace of our old age in any number of ways. The battle is harsher for those who are young. We ourselves have known this fight and have passed through it. . . . Keep up your fight and hope for the victory.[7]

One thing we have to bear in mind is the fact that, in the Christian view of life, love and the cross are intimately bound together. This is so not only because Jesus taught us this, but particularly because he practiced what he preached: *"There is no greater love than this: to lay down one's life for one's friends. You are my friends if you do what I command you."*[8] The supreme sign of God's love for us is seen precisely in the offering that Jesus made of himself on the cross to redeem us.

The Christian Looks to the Cross

Nowadays, people seem to shy away from the cross and mortification more than ever. Of course, the cross has never been very popular. Yet it has undoubtedly given great comfort and strength to those who have been nailed to it by suffering and sorrow, as they find themselves in this way identifying so closely with Christ.[9] Most of us prefer to emphasize the resurrection, with its aspects of joy, glory, praise, freedom and conquest. And this is a very natural reaction: who would not prefer to reach the glory of the Lord without passing through the pain and ignominy of Good Friday? Yet Jesus himself warns us: *"Unless the grain of wheat falls to the earth and dies, it remains just a grain of wheat. But if it dies, it produces much fruit."*[10]

Probably what a lot of people rebel against today is what appears to be a negative, almost anti-Christian approach to the cross, which may have existed sometime in the past: discipline for the sake of discipline, sacrifice which had lost its meaning, forms of moritification which seem very out of place now that we have a better understanding and appreciation of our total nature and of the intimate union of body and soul. However, we must be very careful not to let possible errors of the past obscure the important place of the cross in the Christian life. If we were to try to neglect the cross, we would find ourselves on a collision course with a basic teaching of the Gospel.

What needs to be emphasized, then, is the positive side of the cross, its real purpose in life: to help us grow to the fullest expression of that love and service, which it has come to represent through the death of Jesus. Genuine love leads a person willingly to do whatever is necessary in order to please the beloved or to possess the object loved. This is the only way to understand the following two brief parables of the Lord concerning the kingdom of God:

> The reign of God is like a buried treasure which a man found in
> a field. He hid it again, and rejoicing at his find went and sold
> all he had and bought that field. Or again, the kingdom of
> heaven is like a merchant's search for fine pearls. When
> he found one really valuable pearl, he went back and put up for
> sale all that he had and bought it.[11]

No price, in other words, is too great for those who are convinced that they have found something very valuable and worth possessing. Equally, no price is too great for those who really love Jesus and want to follow him more closely. To possess anything that is good and worthwhile, something beyond the reach of money, demands a concentrated and sustained effort. For some reason or other, however, many seem to hesitate when it comes to believing that the life of the Spirit may also require a similar sustained effort, as well as self-discipline and self-sacrifice. Jesus has not made a mystery of how we can, indeed must, follow him:

> If anyone wishes to come after me, he must deny his very self, take up
> his cross, and begin to follow in my footsteps.[12]

And again, following up on his statement that the grain of wheat must die in order to produce fruit, Jesus adds:

The man who loves his life loses it, while the man who hates his life in this world preserves it to life eternal. If anyone would serve me, let him follow me; where I am, there will my servant be. If anyone serves me, him the Father will honor.[13]

To follow in the footsteps of another is to be that person's disciple. The footsteps of Jesus, however, are indelibly marked by self-sacrificing love:

Such as my love has been for you, so must your love be for each other. This is how all will know you for my disciples: by your love for one another.[14]

The Way to Interior Freedom

The formula, then, that Jesus spells out is really very simple: deny yourself, take up your cross, and follow me, that is, *love as I have loved*. No one, however, is going to be able to love as Jesus did without accepting those pre-conditions of self-denial and taking up the cross, because the love promoted by Jesus is radically opposed to that other, very attractive love, which the materialistic forces around us promote:

Two kinds of love beget two communities [cities]: self-love carried to the point of rejection of God, which is the worldly community; and love of God realized to the point of abandonment of self-sufficiency, which is the heavenly community.[15]

Authors of the spiritual life emphasize in our own times, as they have done also in the past, how self-discipline, no matter the name by which it may be called — penance, mortification, asceticism — is absolutely necessary if we are to enjoy the gift of interior freedom. Such freedom allows us to affirm in ourselves and propose to those around us the true values of life, which are also the gifts of the Spirit: "*love, joy, peace, patient*

*endurance, kindness, generosity, faith, mildness and chastity.
Against such there is no law!"*[16]   If we do not acquire this interior
freedom, we will remain slaves to our own egos, completely
self-centered, in love only with ourselves and our own will.[17]

> To love oneself is to want to do one's own will. Put the will of God
> before all this; learn really to love yourself by overcoming self-love.[18]

A Christian sense of self-discipline or mortification allows
us to see that many attitudes which prevail in our society are
built on false assumptions, which constitute a practical denial of
the spiritual reality of our nature.[19]   By following Christ we are
empowered to seek the true and lasting values of life, which are
totally in accord with our Christian calling.

An Augustinian View of the Cross

In the light of all this, Augustine's very personalistic and
well-balanced approach to the cross, penance and mortification
can be a great aid in understanding what Jesus himself teaches on
these matters.

In general, Augustine tells all Christians that they can only
live up to their name and their vocation if they do not refuse to
walk in the way of Christ by accepting suffering, as Jesus did:
"This is a hard way," he will admit, *"but a safe one."*[20]   Despite
the fact that this statement may sound a bit harsh, it is not so
when seen in the context of Augustine's preaching and teaching.
In fact, his approach to penance and mortification was both new
and moderate, stressing as it did three things: 1) personal
responsibility;   2) the health of the individual;   3) above all
growth in love, unity and interior freedom as a consequence of
asceticism. Augustine had been deeply impressed by the rigor-
ous, prolonged fasts of the monks in the monasteries he visited
in Rome and Milan,[21] but perhaps his own physical

infirmities made him place much more emphasis on other aspects of the penitential life, which were certainly far more important. This becomes clear in the following excerpt:

> With all this [fasting], no one is pressed to endure hardships for which he is unfit. Nothing is imposed on anyone against his will. . . . All their endeavors are concerned not about the rejection of various foods as unclean, but about the subjection of inordinate desire and the maintenance of brotherly love. . . . Charity especially is guarded: food is subservient to charity, speech to charity, customs to charity, facial expressions to charity. Everything works together for charity alone.[22]

Augustine transferred to his religious ideal this simple, basic attitude toward penance, where none are forced against their will, each one is the final judge of how far health can tolerate such practices, and charity is laid down as the ultimate norm for all things. As he says in his *Rule*: *"Let the abiding virtue of charity prevail in all things that minister to the fleeting necessities of life."*[23]

Following Christ's Example

How, then, according to Augustine, are we to respond to the challenge of Jesus to deny ourselves, take up our cross and follow him? Augustine comments on these expressions on many different occasions, but in summary, and in a very down-to-earth way, he says this. For the love of Christ we must: 1) bear up under the various ways in which the world tries to turn us aside from our faith; 2) put up with all that is troublesome; 3) keep the commandments; 4) be motivated by mercy and love as Christ himself was; 5) trust not in ourselves but in Christ; 6) carry the cross of our mortality — this is, our flesh — and keep it subservient to our higher goals; 7) most of all, we must *carry one*

*another's burdens mutually, for this constitutes the perfect fulfillment
of the law of Christ.*

That's quite a program, especially when we consider that
most of these ideas were suggested first of all to the laity. But
quite truthfully, says Augustine, it is the entire Church which is
called to follow Christ. When Christ speaks of the need of
denying oneself and following him, he is not addressing himself
just to virgins, religious and the clergy, but also to the married, to
widows, to all the laity.[24]

The best way to appreciate Augustine's forcefulness in all
this is to let him speak for himself:

> What does it mean, "Let him take up his cross?" Put up with all that is
> annoying: that is how he must follow me. To tell the truth, when he
> follows me, imitating my conduct and keeping my commandments,
> he will have many who will try to oppose him, forbid him, dissuade
> him, and this will be done by those same people who appear to be
> followers of mine. . . . If you want to follow me, you must look on
> all these things . . . as a cross: you will have to endure them, put up
> with them and not give in to them.[25]

> Let them deny themselves, that is, not put their trust in themselves;
> let them take up their cross, that is put up with all the affronts of
> the world for the love of Christ. . . . Persist, persevere, endure, bear
> up under the delay: in this way you will bear your cross.[26]

> That cross of ours which the Lord commands us to carry . . . what
> else is it if not the mortality of our flesh? It distresses us until death is
> swallowed up in victory. Therefore, it is precisely this cross [this flesh
> of ours] which we must crucify and pierce with the nails of the fear of
> God, so that we will be able to carry it freely when it resists us.[27]

When we follow Christ, we seek his interests and his ways, not
our own.[28]   And what are Christ's interests? None other than
the fulfillment of the two great commandments of love:

> This is the law of Christ, that we carry one another's burdens mutually. When we love Christ, it is easy to put up with the other person's weakness, even when we do not love him yet for his good qualities.[29]

Experience readily teaches that the occasions for having to bear with one another's weaknesses will never be absent as long as we live. There is, therefore, no need for those who live in community to ask themselves how they may follow Christ more closely. Their basic penance and mortification is already cut out for them. Just let them be generous in the living of their community life, and they will certainly draw much closer to Christ.[30]

But as Augustine says, the flesh — our mortal nature — is our real cross. It needs to be curbed and tamed if we are to grow in love and be able to set Christ's interests before our own. We must put up a good fight against the temptations which confront us daily and we must overcome them, though by ourselves, this is well beyond our strength:

> Our work in this life is to mortify the works of the flesh by the spirit, to chasten them daily, lessen them, restrain them, put them to death. . . . In this battle, while we labor, we appeal to God for help.[31]

In a passage in his *Confessions*, Augustine gives voice to one of his own struggles, which perhaps many of us could identify with:

> I struggle each day against concupiscence in eating and drinking. It is not something that I can resolve to cut off once and for all and touch no more, as I could concubinage. The bridle put upon the throat must be held with both moderate looseness and moderate firmness. Who is it, Lord, who is not carried a little beyond the limits of his need?[32]

In the same breath that he postulates a moderately relaxed approach, he also insists on moderate firmness. A healthy balance in this sector of life is just as important as in others. What Augustine is saying is that we should so nourish the body that it be of good service, and so restrain it that it not impede our total growth in the Christian life.[33]

Penance Must Lead to Love

But the fact that Augustine always requires moderation and a healthy balance must not make us think that he was opposed to those forms of penance and mortification especially recommended by the Scriptures and by the early Fathers of the Church: prayer, fasting, almsgiving. Not only was he not opposed, he actually spoke frequently of their necessity, always pointing out, however, that their ultimate goal had to be growth in love and harmony. In his letter to Proba, Augustine combines in one short paragraph much of what he holds as important in taking up the cross: on the one hand, the need for prayer, fasting and other types of penance; and on the other hand, the need for personal discernment as to one's capacity for these practices. But above all these things he insists on the preservation of love:

> Prayer is greatly aided by fasting, vigils and every kind of bodily chastisement. Let each one of you do what she can. If one can [only] do less, let her do what she can, so long as she loves in the other what she herself does not do, because she cannot. Thus the weaker will not hold back the stronger, and the stronger will not press the weaker. You owe your conscience to God; but to no one else do you owe anything more except that you love one another.[34]

Almsgiving and prayer, good works and forgiveness of others' offenses, make us so pleasing to God that, when offered with the right dispositions, they wash away all our lesser sins.[35]   One particularly fine piece of advice that Augustine has left us points out how useless fasting or other works of penance are if they are not accompanied by works of love and justice:

If you were immoderately severe toward your servant, your fast
would be rejected. Will it be approved if you fail to acknowledge your
brother? I am not asking what food you abstain from, but what you
love. . . . Do you love justice? . . . Well, then, let your justice be seen. I
think it is only right that you serve what is greater, so that what is
lesser may serve you."[36]

Advice to Religious on Carrying the Cross

1) ADVICE FROM THE RULE

What Augustine has expressed in his teaching to the
people, he repeats to his religious. Quite frankly, the *Rule* speaks
with the greatest simplicity of penance, giving only one concrete
norm: *"Subdue the flesh . . . by fasting and abstinence from food and
drink."* But Augustine immediately adds to this norm an important, qualifying condition: *"Do this,"* he says, *"insofar as your
health permits!"*[37]   There would certainly be no purpose in
doing penance if illness were going to arise from it. The object of
penance in any form is not to injure ourselves, but to make it
easier to achieve that total harmony within ourselves, that
proper priority between body and spirit, which will redound to
the health of our whole being.[38]   As an early follower of
Augustine put it: *"Illness that comes from abstinence merits accusa-
tion rather than reward."*[39]

Augustine goes on to indicate how even those who cannot
remain without some food until the main meal (which was
usually taken in mid-afternoon, around 3 o'clock) should only
take a light snack beforehand, around noon.[40]   The sick however, were freed from any obligation to fast during their illness.
But just as Augustine was eager to provide the sick with special
care so that they could more quickly recover their strength, so
also did he expect them to be mature and responsible enough to
know when that special care should cease. His mind was that

they should return to that simpler mode of life which is more fitting for the servants of God. In other words, religious must be careful not to pamper themselves, prolonging their cure even after they have regained their former health: *"They must not become slaves to the enjoyment of food which was necessary to sustain them in their illness."*[41]

This is the sum of what Augustine has to say explicitly about penance and mortification in the *Rule*. Nevertheless, in several other chapters of the *Rule* a mortified conduct is also implied and even at times demanded of the brothers and sisters. For example, in making sure that their external conduct (clothing, demeanor, behavior, etc.) does not offend anyone;[42]   in avoiding curiosity of the eyes in the presence of the opposite sex;[43]   in overcoming a certain hesitancy or fear to engage in fraternal correction;[44]   in sharing all in common (which can be a real penance);[45]   in seeking forgiveness from those they have offended;[46]   and even in their very attitude towards keeping the *Rule*, which demands that they be watchful in order not to fall:

> But when one of you finds that he has failed on any point, let him
> be sorry for the past, be on his guard for the future, praying that he
> will be forgiven his fault and not be led into temptation.[47]

2) ADVICE TO OTHER RELIGIOUS

In his early years as a bishop, Augustine had occasion to write to a certain Abbot Eudoxius and his brother religious on the island of Capraria, in the Balearic chain, to answer some questions they had proposed to him. In this letter he pointed out several penitential practices which, he said, they should engage in enthusiatically, though always for the glory of God. However, he makes special mention of one action in particular, which underlines once again what we have already observed as his most important concern: *"Above all bear with one another in love — for truly, what could that person put up with who cannot bear with his brother?"*[48]   Loving our brothers and sisters, bearing up with their difficulties and weaknesses, is the acid test of our willingness to bring heart and spirit into subjection to God, which is the whole purpose of penance and mortification. Nothing can better prove our acceptance of the will of God in our lives than fulfilling the two great commandments of love.

3) THE EXAMPLE OF AUGUSTINE'S LIFE

Possidius gives us other insights into Augustine's daily life with the brothers, and how simple and mortified they were in their eating and drinking at the common table. But even here, the author underlines that Augustine would interrupt their normal and rather austere diet for the sake of visitors or those who were ill, offering them meat along with their vegetables and wine. Reading and discussion at table were more important to him than eating and drinking. But he also insisted that all present abstain from superfluous and harmful chatter — which is still another sign of his own mortified conduct, and that which he expected of those who lived with him.[49]   Perhaps most significant of all in Augustine's personal outlook on penance is what Possidius recounts concerning his last illness:

> When speaking with us in a familiar way, it was usual for Augustine to say that once baptism was received, not even those Christians and priests who were highly respected should die without doing good and suitable penance. In his last illness, he himself acted in this way. He had the penitnetial psalms of David written down and fixed to the wall, so that though in bed sick, he could see and read them, while weeping all the time warm tears.[50]

Summing Up

From what we have seen concerning Augustine's thought and actions, it seems clear enough that his attitude towards bearing the cross, that is, toward doing necessary penance and practicing mortification in the Christian life, did not vary to any significant degree, either when he was talking to the laity or to religious. He always insisted on these same points: 1) the necessity of taking up the cross and following Christ; 2) the need for safeguarding one's health while doing this; 3) the presence of a personal sense of responsibility, guided by generosity and prudent moderation; 4) the absolute importance in this, as in all other things, of love as the ultimate norm. If this final norm cannot be achieved, if the unity of a community is disrupted or placed in real danger by what an individual or group may be doing, then this cannot be a wholesome way of imitating Christ.

> The labor of those who love is in no way burdensome; in fact, it even gives pleasure. . . . what matters is what is loved. When we do what we love, either we do not notice the work, or the work itself is loved.[51]

If such is the Augustinian way of carrying the cross, is there anyone who cannot bear this cross with love? At times it seems that, in the wake of the Second Vatican Council, for far too many religious, penance and mortification have suffered a similar fate as meditative and contemplative prayer. Because this kind of prayer was frequently no longer practiced in common, many simply ignored or neglected it. Yet just as religious cannot grow without the prayer of quiet, so they cannot hope to fulfill their goal of following Christ more closely unless they are also willing to take up their cross.

This cross, as we have seen, is multifaceted. It is at one time prayer, fasting and abstinence. It is also, however, dedication to study, and to other forms of the apostolate, undertaken only to seek the interests of Christ. It means bearing up under the trials of daily life, keeping the commandments, being motivated as Jesus was. It means helping to carry one another's burdens, out of love. It means accepting not only the joys of community life, but also its sufferings — the pains and struggles of our brothers and sisters, as well as our own. In all these ways we become more conformed to the image of Jesus Christ, whose cross we were and still are, by our sinfulness and frequent unwillingness to renew ourselves in the Spirit. When we carry our crosses, not only individually, but also as community, they become much lighter, especially when, as Augustine emphasizes time and time again, they lead us to greater unity and love. The following quotation sums up Augustine's attitude and can serve as a fitting conclusion to these reflections.

> If you hold on to the words of Christ . . . you will not become enslaved either by the desires of the flesh, or by those of the eyes, or by worldly ambition. And you will make room for the coming of charity, so that you may love God. . . . Each one is what he loves. Do you love the earth? You will be earthy. Do you love God? What shall I say: that you will be God? I would not dare say it on my own authority, but listen to the Scriptures: 'I said, you are gods and sons of the Most High.'[52]

7

CLOTHE YOURSELVES WITH HUMILITY

CHRISTIANITY IS A RELIGION OF CONTRASTS, sometimes of stark contrasts, which cannot be understood from a purely human point of view. Those who walk in the light, or in grace, are contrasted with those who walk in the darkness, that is, in sin, or without faith.[1]   Life is contrasted with death, so much so that those who die will live, while those who want to save their lives will lose them.[2]   It is said that the first will be last, and the last first;[3]   that those who exalt themselves will be humbled while the humble shall be raised up.[4]   Moreover, the poor will be filled and the rich will be sent away empty.[5]   Indeed, the priorities that Jesus teaches are diametrically opposed to what the world holds dear, goals such as being first, being rich, being self-made, living for the here and now without thought or provision for the hereafter.

One other contrast in the Scriptures, which is worthy of special note, is the frequently repeated opposition expressed between weakness and strength, which affects not only human beings, but strangely enough, even God himself. This becomes particularly clear in the following examples taken from St. Paul:

> "My grace is enough for you," said Jesus to Paul, "for in weakness power reaches perfection. . . . Therefore," says Paul, "I am content with weakness . . . for when I am powerless, it is then that I am strong."[6]
>
> The message of the cross is complete absurdity to those who are headed for ruin, but to us who are experiencing salvation it is the power of God. . . . [Christ crucified] is a stumbling block to Jews, and an absurdity to Gentiles, but to those who are called, Jews and Greeks alike, Christ [is] the power of God and the wisdom of God. . . . God chose those whom the world considers absurd to shame the wise; he singled out the weak of this world to shame the strong.[7]

Pride: the Fundamental Sin

There is a profound bit of theology hidden in these phrases: weakness is turned into strength, worldly wisdom into foolishness in the presence of God, and the helplessness of a crucified Man-God into the very wisdom and power of God conquering death. This theology still constitutes a language that is an "absurdity" to those who have no faith, in our generation as in Paul's times.

How can one explain this teaching to those who feel that what really counts in this world is pushing oneself ahead, no matter how many others get stepped on? Or to those who trust so much in human reasoning and the wisdom of science that they give little or no credence to the wisdom of God and his Church? Or to those who consider themselves self-made persons, superior to all others, who have faith only in what they can see, feel or measure? The pride that underlies such attitudes has even been known to produce religious zealots, as in the case of St. Paul before his conversion; or as in the similar case of Augustine, who proselytized so fervently in his early Manichean days.

It was pride that for so long kept Augustine from entering the Church. No wonder he understood its subtle workings so well. He was well qualified to warn his people of its destructive effects and to encourage them to imitate Christ in his humility. And there can be no question that he particularly emphasized humility as one of the foundations of the religious life.

Augustine's Encounter with Pride

Augustine well knew the power of pride: it could wreck a person's life. It had almost wrecked his! Had he not exaggerated his sins before the companions of his youth in order to appear more daring in their sight?[8]

More importantly, had he not closed himself to the message of salvation in the Scriptures because it was not couched in the literary style of the classical authors he knew and esteemed so much?[9]   He felt the Scriptures were "beneath his dignity," and that, as a result, he could learn nothing worthwhile from them. Did he not go to hear St. Ambrose preach because of his rhetorical abilities, rather than because of what he might learn from him as a man of God?[10]   Did he not have occasion to experience through his own flock and clergy, and almost in his own body, the violence that can arise from pride, especially ideological pride, such as was manifested by the religious fanaticism of the Donatists and Circumcellions, who were the terrorists of those times?[11]   Moreover, in his pastoral relations with his people, as well as with those who entered the religious life, he spoke openly and frequently of the dangers which this sin brought to the human race. No wonder, then, that he stressed the need for humility among all who wished to follow Christ.

A Humble Heart Draws God to Itself

Time and again he stressed that the primary reason why Christians had to be humble was that they might thereby better imitate their Father in heaven, who for the sake of all became humble in Jesus Christ. And in proving his point he often made use of the same concepts employed by the Scriptures when they contrast strength and weakness, pride and humility, casting down the mighty and lifting up the lowly:

> Perhaps you would be ashamed to imitate a humble man; at least imitate a humble God.[12]

> If in your weakness you do not spurn the humble Christ, you will remain truly steadfast in the exalted Christ. For what was the purpose of Christ's becoming humble if not because you were weak?[13]

> The prouder a person's heart, the further it moves away from God, and if it moves away from God, it descends into the depths. A humble heart, on the contrary, draws God near it from heaven.[14]

What Augustine says in this last text is something which may perhaps be illustrated from our own personal experience. It is easy, for example, to give gifts to the poor, who are in need of nearly everything. But it is next to impossible to find a gift for the rich, who already have everything they need and much more besides, or to help the self-made person, who wants to do everything by him- or herself. So it is with God: he can easily fill the humble person or help the needy, those, that is, who acknowledge their innate weakness. But God can only be a beggar, so to speak, at the doorstep of the proud. The proud person's declaration of strength brings out the weakness of God. God allows himself to become almost helpless in such a case, because he will not force himself or his graces on anyone. The only way in which God can help people overcome pride is by bringing them to such straits that they are forced to recognize their real weaknesses:

> All proud people claim to be strong. . . . Therefore, in his goodness, God's first grace is to bring us to admit our weakness, to confess that whatever good we do and whatever ability we have is due to him.[15]

Augustine adds another very incisive thought when he says that the proud do not want to claim as their leader a God who is weak. Such a God is a scandal to them because he was born as a man, hungered, thirsted, grew weary and finally was crucified — and all these are signs of weakness, helplessness, and dependence on others, which the proud are unwilling to admit in themselves and much more unwilling to find in God.[16]   But, continues Augustine, God lowered himself and became weak like us and for us, because otherwise we would have been incapable of reaching him. The humility of the God-man Jesus, then, is the only medicine capable of healing our pride, but not even this medicine is available to us unless we are willing to recognize the reality of our sinful condition and weakness, admit that we are ill, and by that very fact, open ourselves to be healed.[17]   It is just as Jesus said: *"People who are in good health do not need a doctor; sick people do. . . . I have come to call, not the self-righteous, but sinners."*[18]

The Heart of Humility

But if pride is the failure to acknowledge the role of God in our lives, to see ourselves as his gift, and is the tendency to set ourselves up as the independent center of everything, how can we understand humility? First of all, for Augustine humility does not consist in putting ourselves down, having a poor self-image of ourselves, failing to appreciate or develop our God-given talents and other gifts. Augustine even accuses people who act like immature adults "milk drinkers" instead of mature adults who take solid food to nourish themselves and make progress in their faith.[19] His description of humility is simple and straightforward:

> No one is telling you: 'Be less than you are'; but 'know what you are'; know that you are weak, know that you are a man, know yourself a sinner. Know that it is he [God] who frees you from blame; know that you are tarnished. Let your confession reveal the stain of your heart, and you will belong to the flock of Christ.[20]

Such an attitude in no way demeans an individual; rather it brings out his or her true value as a masterwork and gift of God. As Augustine comments elsewhere:

> If you praise the works of God, then you will also have to praise yourself, for you too are a work of God.... Look, here is how you can at the same time praise yourself and not be proud. Praise not yourself, but God in you. Offer praise, not because you are this or that kind of a person, but because God made you; not because you are capable of doing this or that, but because he works in you and through you.[21]

These basic ideas on pride and humility Augustine shared constantly with his people. How he applied them to those living in his religious community becomes quite clear when we take a closer look at some of the matters he touched upon in his *Rule*.

Pride and Humility at Work in the Monastery

One of the best known and most explicit passages of the *Rule* which deals with pride and its counterpart, humility, occurs in the first chapter. With complete impartiality, Augustine speaks of the two principal classes of people who composed the society of his time and provided most of the candidates for the religious life: the very poor and the rich or well-born. He put both groups on their guard about the dangers of pride and the consequent need for humility. The poor are to avoid "*holding their heads high,*"[22] metaphorically speaking, because they now associate with people whom they could not have approached while living in the world. The rich, on the other hand, must not "*look down*" on these poor persons whom they may have completely disdained in their former social life.[23]   The fact of the matter is that their common calling to the religious life has now brought very close together these two classes who were quite distant from one another in civilian life, so close, in fact, that they are to become one in mind and in heart as they journey toward God.[24]

Those who were poor are invited to lift up toward God, not their heads, but their hearts, which is clearly the attitude of a humble person; and those who were rich are invited to rejoice, not because of their wealthy origins, but because of their fellowship with those coming from a poorer condition in life — also clearly an attitude of humility. The appeal to both groups is directed toward bringing about that change of mentality, insisted upon by Jesus, which puts things in their proper perspective with relation to the kingdom.

But if social origins or rank can be one cause of pride, Augustine was quick to point out that for these same persons there is another, more subtle source of pride. He sees this developing in those who come from a condition of poverty. They can become too comfortable and "puffed up" with pride in the religious life, because they now possess things which they could not have enjoyed before. Those who were well off, on the other hand, may well lose all the merit gained by the sharing of their wealth with the community if they take more pride in doing this than if they had enjoyed their riches in secular life. Indeed, what good does it do to become poor by giving to the monastery, if this is going to make the rich person proud? It is here that

Augustine underlines a perennially valid reality of life which should keep us always on guard: *"Pride lurks even in good works, seeking to destroy them."*[25] In brief, we are cautioned to remember that neither social status nor material goods, nor the lack of them, makes one immune to the subtle attacks of pride. We remain very human, even in the religious life, and we are continually in need of learning from the humility of Jesus.

Drawing Some Practical Conclusions

If we take a look at some of the circumstances surrounding religious life today, we can draw some practical conclusions about what Augustine says concerning the danger of pride and the real need for humility. This may also help us discern just how much we have actually learned from the example of Jesus' humility, and how far we still have to go in this regard.

1) PRIDE OF ORIGINS

A marked change in the social mentality of our times — at least in the more developed countries — as compared to when Augustine lived, almost precludes any danger of pride arising nowadays because of association in the community with those whom we would not have approached normally in the world. In our times there is very little left of the class distinctions that existed even one hundred years ago. And yet experience teaches that other, similar forms of pride can and perhaps do exist.

In certain parts of the world, for example, religious (or seminarians) can suddenly find themselves on a higher rung of society by the very fact of responding to the Lord's call. There is nothing wrong with this in itself. In fact it can be a means of being better able to serve others. But the temptation can thereby arise of feeling oneself "superior" to those who have been left behind at home, so much so that these religious begin to feel they should be treated differently: with greater deference, better living conditions and other special privileges. This same temptation of feeling oneself "superior" can be experienced also in the area of racial or ethnic discrimination. The problems of society all too easily find their way into the religious life of today, just as they did in Augustine's time.[26]

2) Pride of Personal Talents

Pride, however, can enter the religious life in even more subtle ways. There are other kinds of wealth, much more valuable than that represented by material possessions: the talents and gifts of each individual, for example, which are also to be shared with the community, can easily give rise to pride. Some have a great wealth of intellectual or academic skills; others have their wealth in technical or manual skills, in social graces, in a heightened psychological acumen, in the way they easily deal with people and relate to others. Those who possess such gifts can fall into the same trap of pride that Augustine speaks about in the first chapter of the *Rule*, the trap: of "looking down" on others who don't possess such gifts themselves.

This can be seen at times through the impatience and irritation shown because others are slower; it can be seen in those who consider themselves more important or even irreplaceable in their present assignments. Some may even reach such extreme positions that they refuse interiorly to accept what others have to offer, simply because they don't believe that others have anything worthwhile to share with them. They close themselves to learning from their less-gifted brothers or sisters, thinking in their hearts: What good can come from them? What do they know about these things? It is the same attitude some people took toward Jesus in his own day, asking themselves: What good can come out of Nazareth? In much the same way some wealthier nations may treat poorer ones, doling out funds and know-how, maybe even exploiting them, but rarely attempting, or even expecting, to learn anything in return from the people of these countries.

How absurd it would be to enter the religious life, make all the sacrifices relative to such a challenge, present oneself to the Church as a committed Christian, perform a very good work in the sight of God — and then allow pride to gnaw away at this generous self-offering to the extent that it becomes self-seeking or a self-centered affair? Quite truthfully we can still ask: Have things changed so much since Augustine's times? Not so much, I would venture. We still have a lot to learn from the humility of Christ, as Augustine points out in this passage:

> We are heading toward great things. Let us take advantage of the little things and we will become great. Do you want to reach the heights of God? First take hold of the humility of God. . . . Put on the humility of Christ. Learn to be humble, do not grow proud. . . . Look at a tree: first it seeks the depths, so that it may grow to the heights. It puts its roots into the ground so that its treetops may reach toward the heavens. Is it not grounded in humility?[27]

A Heart That Feigns Ignorance

Augustine is quite explicit in the first chapter of his *Rule* concerning pride and humility, as we have seen. But he also refers implicitly to proud or humble attitudes in religious in several other places of that *Rule*.[28]   I would like to mention one of these attitudes in particular, so that being better aware of it, we can deal with it more effectively in our own lives and in our communities.

In chapter four of the *Rule* Augustine is concerned principally with how religious should safeguard their chastity. Eager also to safeguard the good reputation of one who may be accused of some failing in this regard, Augustine proposes a very discreet method of correction. However, if this private correction fails its purpose, the matter is to be brought to the attention of others. When is such a step to be taken? A meaningful translation of Augustine's thought on this matter would read this way: "*Should he/she feign ignorance, the others are to be summoned.*"[29]   "Feigning ignorance" is an act which betrays a proud heart, a heart that knows it is wrong, but is unwilling to acknowledge this fact. It is a heart prepared to perpetrate a sham, hoping to get away with it. It is not very encouraging to think that there may be a few religious of this stamp even today, just as apparently there were sixteen centuries ago.

But let me mention some other more common ways of "feigning ignorance," which reveal at least a subconscious attitude of pride, and which can be very detrimental for community living.

How many of us, for example, have ever met religious who act as though they can never make a mistake, can never be wrong? Theoretically, of course, they will admit they can err, but in practice an admission of failure is next to impossible: some excuse will always be made to cancel out responsibility. These people cannot bring themselves to admit that they, too, are subject to that universal condition which is nicely summed up in the old saying: "To err is human, to forgive divine." In a similar vein we sometimes find others who are unable to accept criticism of almost any kind, be it from their peers, from their superiors, or from the people they serve. Fr. Bernard Häring rightly labels this attitude for what it really is: pride.

> Part of the humble service of the word of God is readiness to accept possible failure. The fear of blame or criticism is another form of vanity.[30]

Fighting the Good Fight

It is very hard to know ourselves well. How much harder to know the virtues and talents of others! This alone should put us on our guard, make us beware of becoming "puffed up" with pride, of considering ourselves "superior." Our very human condition underlines more than ever the need we have of the Lord and of one another in our struggle to live a good life. Moreover, we cannot fight with our own strength alone. We need the strength that God gives us, for as Paul puts it, *"our battle is not against human forces but . . . against the rulers of this world of darkness."*[31]   Augustine challenges us in the same way:

> Fight, that you may overcome. Overcome, that you may be crowned. Be humble, lest you fall in battle.[32]

A modern spiritual writer uses similar terminology, pointing out how the very trials of our spiritual life constitute the battleground on which we must prove ourselves and acquire true humility:

> Humility is attained only in battle. . . . The importance of tribulations in your spiritual life lies in the fact that only through such trials do you acquire true humility. You see clearly the futility of your own efforts and the importance of God becoming your Savior. . . . Pride is the ultimate temptation that is never really conquered.[33]

There are indeed many advantages in imitating the humility of Christ: God draws nearer to us, we learn to live peacefully and joyfully in community and among others, and we discover how to use our talents for the common good. When we humble ourselves before the Lord, he will lift us up.[34]   In this light, it is no wonder that Augustine insists so much on humility as a companion that must always remain at our side as we go through life. It is no wonder that for him, and for his followers, humility is one of the firm foundations on which the community is built and through which it can grow. The following quotation, taken from one of Augustine's letters, speaks for itself in bringing these thoughts to a reflective conclusion:

> My wish is that you submit to (Jesus) with your whole heart . . . and provide no other way for yourself to firmly grasp the truth than what he himself provides who, as God, saw the weakness of our footsteps. That way, moreover, consists first, of humility, second, of humility, third, of humility. And as often as you would ask me, I would repeat this same advice. It is not that there are no other precepts to be spoken of. But, unless humility precede, accompany and follow up all the good we accomplish, unless we keep our eyes fixed on it, stay close to it and are restrained by it, even as we rejoice over some good thing we have done, pride will snatch everything right out of our hands.[35]

8

AS THOSE LIVING IN FREEDOM, UNDER GRACE

THE *Rule of St. Augustine* concludes with an impressive exhortation which asks the Lord to grant those who follow it the grace of being able to observe its precepts in the spirit of love, *"not as slaves living under the law, but as those living in freedom under grace."*[1]   In this particular phrase an unmistakable contrast is spelled out between a pre-Christian mentality — identified with slavery and the law — and that mentality inspired by the coming of Jesus — identified with freedom and grace.

Love, not Fear

By his life and teaching Jesus showed both Jew and Gentile that God was not a scowling ruler waiting to catch them in their weakness and punish them, but a loving Father who cared immensely for them. Consequently, their relationship with him was to be based on a similar response in love. Jesus himself was living proof of the Father's love. He asked no more of his followers than he had already asked of himself: a love that accepted people where they were and at the same time looked to the future to see what they could yet become by growing in God's grace.

In this same vein Jesus also made it clear that the relationship of those in authority with those subject to them was to be completely different from what took place among the authorities of those times, who liked to appear important and lord it over their subjects:

> It cannot be like that with you. Anyone among you who aspires to greatness must serve the rest; whoever wants to rank first among you must serve the needs of all. The Son of Man has not come to be served but to serve — to give his life in ransom for the many.[2]

That this is not a very popular approach to things even in our own day can be best illustrated by an incident that happened to me some years back when I was Prior General of the Augustinians. I was visiting one of our minor seminaries in Spain, and as was my custom I gathered the 250 students of this particular seminary in their auditorium so I could speak to them all at once. When I had finished my short talk I opened the floor to any questions these young lads (11-18 years of age) might care to ask me about the Augustinians. Things got off to a good start: one asked how many Augustinians there were in the world, another was concerned with the type of work we did, and still another wanted to know in what nations we worked.

Having cleared away these questions with little difficulty, a small hand went up way in the back of the room. I recognized him and got this most unexpected question: "Father General," he asked, "What do I have to do to become General of the

Augustinians?" Well, as you can understand, the place fairly broke up with laughter, followed by lots of applause. I invited this young man to come to the front with me, where I discovered he was only 11 years old and had just arrived at the seminary. Then I looked down at him very seriously and asked: "So you really want to be General of the Augustinians, do you?" "Yes," came the unhesitating reply. "Well, then," I answered, "you must do just as Jesus taught us and become the least of all these companions of yours and the servant of all. Maybe then some day you will be General!" As soon as he heard that he had to be the least and serve everyone else, he made a face depicting great displeasure and decided he wanted nothing more to do with becoming General of the Augustinians. Through the years I followed the growth of this young man, and I am happy to be able to say that he has definitively given up his desire to be worldwide leader of the Augustinians: as of a few years ago he is happily married and already has a child.

Augustine understood the fundamental Christian concept of authority very well; he even incorporated it into his *Rule*. For him authority and obedience were so interrelated through love, that a mutual responsibility was laid upon the shoulders of superiors and other religious alike for the attainment of only one goal: the building up of the community and of each individual in Christ.

But this kind of authority and obedience, inspired by love and not by fear, demands mature and responsible people in the community. It will only work where religious are convinced that their purpose in the consecrated life is to obey, not their own feelings or inclinations, but the law of the Spirit, the law of love, as it is manifested to them through their insertion into a community of faith and love.

Failures of the Past and of the Present

In the decades preceding the Second Vatican Council, the basic ideas of Jesus concerning authority and obedience as a service in love had unfortunately not always been heeded. In some sectors of the Church — and quite naturally in the religious life as well — an atmoshpere had often prevailed that was more reminiscent of the Old Testament than of the New, characterized more by fear and the rule of law than by love and compassion. Looking back, it is really difficult to understand how such a mentality could ever have existed in the light of the teaching of Christ and in the light of the love which Augustine says should characterize the relationship of the superior with the others.

It is no wonder, then, that in some places today obedience in the religious life has fallen on hard times. It is no wonder that it has suffered — in my view — perhaps more than any other element of religious life. It is no wonder that, though the Second Vatican Council reversed this trend with its enlightened teaching,[3]   and though the attitude of those in authority today is, in general, much different than before, still a terrible distrust lingers on in all too many religious. This distrust has not only blinded some to the significant changes already achieved, but most of all it has made it very difficult for them to accept their renewed roles in the community. A false understanding of obedience has been rightly rejected, but unfortunately, in not a few cases, obedience itself has also been effectively rejected with it.

Maybe now, however, we are approaching a time when we can see things more objectively once again. Though some problems undoubtedly still remain, we have also seen notable progress. Renewal, broader consultation, more tolerance of diverse viewpoints, and the revitalized functioning of community meetings where real decisions are made have begun to enhance the exercise of mutual responsibility in many religious families. Yet despite these gains, not all have understood or accepted their full and oftentimes renewed responsibility in the community. Not all, for example, are willing to accept those community decisions in which they themselves cast a dissenting vote. And on the contrary, there are those who will approve matters in these meetings and yet be unwilling to lift a finger to help see that these matters are carried out. Both cases represent examples of a failure to accept corporate responsibility and are often clear signs of immaturity.[4]

Bearing all these things in mind, it can be to our advantage to take a brief look at Augustine's approach to evangelical authority and evangelical obedience. What he says has its relevance even for our changing times. And what he says of religious superiors (or leaders or coordinators as they are called in some groups today) can and should be applied to all those who, though not superiors in the strict sense of the word, still frequently treat with other religious from a certain position of authority. I have in mind especially those in charge of formation, school principals, even pastors and their associates.

1. EVANGELICAL AUTHORITY

What kind of superior was Augustine? What was his approach to his religious in the monastery and to his people in the diocese? How did he deal with erroneous ways of thinking or acting, or correct recalcitrants? How did he react to those who were evidently out of line? What did he himself teach about the duties of those who were placed in positions of leadership: their relationships with those they were called to lead, the responsibility of those who were to obey?

In the matter of authority and obedience we meet in Augustine once again a fine sense of balance. This shows up when he speaks on the subject of homelife in general, about society at large, or about the religious life. He clearly implies, for example, that true peace in any home is achieved only when there is an *"harmonious interplay of authority and obedience among those who live there."* Moreover, in a Christian home *"those who command serve those whom they appear to rule."*⁵ These thoughts recur frequently in Augustine, for the peace he speaks of here is equivalent to that harmony and unity which he expects of those who live together in the religious life.

In what concerns this harmonious interplay of authority and obedience in the religious community the *Rule* is admirable: in very simple terms it lays down what is expected of superiors and sets the tone for the relationship between them and the other members of the community. Practically speaking, Augustine sums up what he expects of superiors in just one paragraph of the *Rule*; anything else he says of them concerns their place in resolving practical matters of distributing goods or caring for the spiritual and physical welfare of the others.

> The superior, for his part, must not think himself fortunate in his exercise of authority but in his role as one serving you in love. In your eyes he shall hold the first place among you by the dignity of his office, but in fear before God he shall be as the least among you. He must show himself an example of good works towards all. Let him "admonish the unruly, cheer the fainthearted, support the weak, and be patient towards all" (1 Th 5:14). Let him uphold discipline while instilling respect for it in others. And though both are necessary, he should strive to be loved by you rather than feared, ever mindful that he must give an account of you to God.⁶

A few ideas stand out in this description: 1) superiors are to serve the others out of love, and strive to be loved more than feared; 2) they are to be guided by a deep humility because of the responsibility entrusted to them; 3) they are to be an example to all; 4) and finally, they are to be properly concerned about keeping good order in the religious house. We can now take a closer look at these four qualities of that person whom Augustine would view as a good superior.

1) SERVING IN LOVE

In Augustine's view the most important quality of superiors is a genuine love for their religious, a love which will motivate them in whatever they are expected to do. Whatever else is demanded of these leaders concerns putting this love into practice: humility, exemplary conduct, correction of those who disturb the community, concern for the weak, and patience towards all. In other words, everything that is basic to living the *Rule* in its entirety is expected equally as much of superiors as of the others: all are called to observe its precepts "*in a spirit of charity.*"[7]   Moreover, since in observing these precepts no one is to act as a "*slave living under the law,*" superiors must take care to treat the religious just as Augustine says: "*as those living in freedom under grace.*"

The idea that superiors not consider themselves happy because they have been given a certain authority fits in very well with Augustine's insistence on this position being one of service in love, a service, moreover, directed not to the good of the superior, but to the common good. Once more, then, we are reminded of a fundamental principle of the Augustinian style of community life by which all the religious, the superior included, will make progress: they are to put the good of the community before their own personal advantage. In his sermon on pastors in the Church, Augustine speaks concretely to this point:

> Since superiors are designated for the purpose of looking out for the good of their subjects, in the fulfillment of their office they should not seek their own advantage but that of their subjects. Whoever is such a superior that he delights in being placed over others, seeks his own honor and looks out only for his own convenience, is fattening himself, not his flock.[8]

2) SERVING WITH HUMILITY

No one can be the servant of others if he or she feels "superior," "above" these others, so to speak. They must have the same attitude that Jesus expected of those who would be first: they must be the least of all![9]   And this simply reiterates the necessity of a superior being humble: humble in the sight of God, humble in the service of the other religious. Augustine was inspired by this very same attitude himself, even as a bishop:

> And yet we, too, who appear to speak to you from a higher place, lie full of fear at your feet, since we know what a severe accounting is to be rendered of this lofty office.[10]

When the community calls some religious to the responsibility of being superiors, it is not with the intent of "honoring" them or placing them "above" the others. Honor may come to them as a result of their election or nomination, but that is certainly not the intent or the criterion for selecting them. The intent is that these religious accept positions of leadership, of special responsibility, of encouragement, so as to guarantee that harmony and unity of mind and heart which are the hallmarks of every Augustinian community. If some were to put on airs because they are now functioning as superiors, we would have to say that they simply have not understood the Gospel message or the spirit of Augustine.

3) AN EXAMPLE TO ALL

Thirdly, superiors are to be an example to all. And that is truly a difficult task, because not all see things in the same light. But at least they must lead the way, ask of others no more than they would ask of themselves, and entrust the community to

God in their prayers. Augustine would probably have applied to superiors what on another occasion he said of the preacher:

> There are a great many who . . . will not listen submissively to that person who does not listen to himself, and they come to despise both the preacher and the Word of God that is preached to them.[11]

When superiors fail to give an example of patience, humility or service, are not the other religious quite likely to begin to look down on what the superiors may be trying to communicate to them? Superiors simply cannot lead religious to the goal of holiness and unity which is proposed in the Gospel (and explicitly in Augustine's *Rule*) unless they themselves are the first to strive for this. Superiors cannot expect obedience from their fellow religious if they themselves are not willing to give such obedience to their *Rule*, Constitutions, and higher superiors. As Augustine puts it: *"What is more unjustifiable than that those who are unwilling to obey their superiors should want to be obeyed by their subordinates?"*[12]   There is something that follows from all this as a natural consequence: superiors are especially obliged to know what is expected of them by their *Rule* and Constitutions, and if they cannot teach their Congregation's spirituality in theory, they should at least strive to teach it by their example.

4) KEEPING GOOD ORDER IN THE COMMUNITY

Finally, Augustine places in the superior's hands an overall concern for the good order of the community. If we had not already seen the tremendous importance Augustine placed on harmony and unity as the principal goals of his community, it might really surprise us to see how much emphasis he puts on this point. Harmony and unity are essential to the growth of the community because they permit it to be more free to search for and find Christ in its midst. On four specific occasions in his brief *Rule* Augustine points out the superior's obligation to correct and even punish, should the offense be sufficiently serious and the offender be adamant in his or her attitudes.[13]

But Augustine does not expect the impossible of his followers. He is very much aware of human frailty among those who have embraced the religious life. And this very fact leads him to remark that, *"Even though good order reigns in my household, I am a man and I live among men."*[14] All of which well explains how Possidius could write of him that he would either censure or tolerate the lack of good order and the infractions committed by the brothers against right conduct, according as either approach was more fitting or necessary.[15] Augustine's prudent approach to such situations can be gathered from these words:

> Let the brethren be admonished by their superiors out of charity, with greater or less severity, in keeping with the different faults.[16]

> But let the superior act well, that is, with humble charity and mild severity, so that he may be mindful that he is the servant of his brethren.[17]

This mildness in severity is brought out again very clearly in Augustine's approach to social evils in general:

> In my opinion it is not by harshness, severity, or overbearing methods that these social evils are removed, but by education rather than by formal commands, by persuasion rather than by threats. This is the way to deal with people in general; severity, however, should be employed only against the sins of the few.[18]

However, none of this should lead superiors to think that they are automatically excused from correcting their religious, should there be a need to do so:

> Evil is actually rendered for evil when one who ought to be admonished is not, and the matter is rather passed over by a perverse bit of pretense.[19]

And so he makes a heartfelt appeal to all:

> If you are our brothers and sisters, our sons and daughters, and if we
> are fellow servants, or rather your servants in Christ, then listen to
> our admonitions, accept our commands, receive our counsel.[20]

This appeal could be followed up by another, which reveals
Augustine's attitude toward all the faithful under his guidance. It
is an attitude that all superiors should certainly want to make
their own in relation to those they serve:

> Let me be helped by your prayers, so that [the Lord] may see fit to
> help me bear his burden. When you pray in this way, it is really for
> yourselves that you are praying. For what is the burden of which I am
> speaking but you? Pray for me, then, as I myself pray that you may
> not be burdensome. . . . Support me so that . . . we may bear one
> another's burdens. In this way we will fulfill the law of Christ.[21]

Concluding these brief insights into the qualities and
characteristics of a good superior we find that we have come
right back to what has been pointed out with insistence elsewhere: namely, it is by bearing one another's burdens — including those of the superior — that we really demonstrate our love
for one another and our sincere desire to follow Christ.[22]

2. EVANGELICAL OBEDIENCE

But if evangelical authority makes such demands on
superiors, evangelical obedience is going to make corresponding
demands on all the religious. It is well to understand that from
Augustine's viewpoint both obedience and authority are ex-
tremely important in order to assure that there be such unity and
harmony in the community that the search for God is favored
and that the pursuit of the common good is placed above

personal advantage. Furthermore, Augustine desires that our living out of the *Rule* not be the result of servile fear, but a practical exercise in love for one's fellow religious, motivated by grace. Because love is the dominant note in the community, it must also be the prevailing characteristic in the relationship between authority and obedience, where it has such practical applications.

Just as we considered the role of the superior under four headings, so also here can we underline four special characteristics that Augustine relates to obedience: 1) Obeying the superior as a father/mother; 2) seeing God in the superior; 3) recognizing a mutual responsibility; 4) accepting correction.

1) OBEYING THE SUPERIOR AS A FATHER/MOTHER

In his early days as a convert, Augustine was very impressed by the saintly and distinguished superiors he had encountered in the Roman communities he visited, so much so that he wrote of them in this fashion:

> These fathers are not only very holy in the way they live, but also outstanding for their holy learning; they excel in all things. Without pride they look out for those whom they call their sons, and while their authority is great in giving orders, great also is the willing obedience of those under their care.[23]

This model of a superior is carried over, but only in part, in what Augustine wrote later on in his *Rule*: *"The superior should be obeyed as a father."*[24]   I have deliberately said "only in part," because it appears quite evident to me that Augustine has not adopted for his followers that more passive type of obedience which he seemed to find in those monasteries he speaks of having visited. As a matter of fact, nowhere in the *Rule* does Augustine speak of the religious as being his sons/daughters or children. Whenever they are addressed, it is as brothers or sisters. Augustine even seems to exclude quite deliberately the type of relationship which would exist between parents and children when he exhorts all to avoid servile fear, and to obey rather as those living in freedom under grace. Such a parent/ child relationship would also be contrary to the entire thrust of the *Rule*, which places so great a responsibility on all the religious to act as adults. This will hopefully become clearer in what follows.

2) SEEING GOD IN THE SUPERIOR

In the same breath in which he says that the superior is to be obeyed as a father or mother, Augustine adds that this is to be done, *"with the respect due him, so as not to offend God in his person."*[25] It would seem that with such words Augustine wanted to emphasize the goal he had already proposed in the beginning of the *Rule*, namely, that all were to honor God in one another, whose temples they had become.[26] This honor toward God present in one another was also, and perhaps especially, to be recognized in the case of the superior. Why this emphasis on the obvious? Could it have been because, with his great practical sense, Augustine foresaw how easy it would be for the religious to forget this fact in the case of the superior? After all, superiors frequently have to deal with the others in such concrete and sometimes painful situations that these could easily be led to criticize or even oppose them if this presence of God were not accentuated. Superiors, then, are also to be the object of our love, care and concern. Most strikingly Augustine urges us to show them merciful compassion, for our own good as well as for theirs. The more we are obedient, the more we show this merciful love:

It is by being obedient, therefore, that you show mercy not only
towards yourselves, but also towards the superior, whose higher
place among you exposes him/her all the more to greater peril.[27]

As Augustine notes elsewhere, it is all too easy to see one's
fellow religious from a merely human vantage point, a fact which
prevents our seeing God in them: *"But if he loved with a spiritual
love this brother whom he sees from a human viewpoint, he would see
God who is love itself."*[28]   We would fall into this very human
way of viewing things, if we only looked to the human qualities
of those leading us, for example, to their ability to speak persua-
sively, without also seeing their authority to teach and direct as
the leaders of the community. For this very reason Augustine
enjoins religious, *"not to look to the skillful style of the one addressing you, but rather to the authority of the one commanding
you."*[29]   The superiors' human frailty is not to get in the way of
our seeing their authority and their right to ask certain things of
us. As one modern spiritual writer has put the same idea:

If you only love someone who is perfect, you love no one. If you only
obey those who are right, you never obey. And if you believe in
something obvious, you do not believe.[30]

Another author, who is an expert on Augustine, emphasizes strongly the place of love and mercy in Augustine's
concept of obedience:

Office [in the *Rule*] is seen completely in the light of love. . . .
Obedience on the part of the community members lies exactly in the
same line. For Augustine, being obedient is primarily an act of love
for another . . . an act of 'merciful love'. . . . Obeying thus becomes a
shared bearing of the burden and care of the whole community. . . . In
a certain sense it is both surprising and enriching that obedience
should be removed from the context of faith, in which it was for
many centuries enclosed, and placed also in the context of love.[31]

3) A MUTUAL RESPONSIBILITY

This approach to obedience fits in very well, once again, with Augustine's insistence on trust in one another, respect for the individual, and at the same time a predominant concern for the common good before personal advantage. It fits in equally with the responsibility placed on the individual, as well as on the superior, to observe the precepts of the *Rule* out of love. It also coincides well with Augustine's Pauline vision of perfect love as being found in those who, in living together, fulfill the law of Christ by bearing one another's burdens.[32] This is also why Augustinian obedience can never be looked upon as something passive, or as something which hinders a person's true growth in a human and Christian way.

In the same fashion, quarreling, murmuring, destructive criticism have no place in the community, much less as a response to what the superior may request. And yet these elements will show up in those who do not make an effort to attain that perfect love of Christ, which consists in honoring him in one another and bearing one another's burdens:

> When those in whom the love of Christ is not perfect come together, they will be hateful, annoy one another, create disturbances, upset the others with their own restlessness, and seek out what they can say about them. . . . All murmurers have been eloquently described somewhere in the Scriptures: 'The heart of the fool is like a cartwheel.' And it can't avoid squeaking. And that is the way it is with many brothers. It is only physically that they live together.[33]

To avoid such a sad state of affairs, Augustine likens religious to ships gathered together in a harbor. He urges them to draw closer together without colliding, and to love one another. To achieve this, he adds, *"Complete impartiality and persevering love are necessary; and when the wind bursts in through the open end of the harbor, prudent piloting must be practiced."*[34]

The reference to the role of the superior and of the entire group is evident here. Perhaps the whole matter is admirably summed up when Augustine counsels: *"Put more effort into seeking agreement among yourselves than in criticizing one another."*[35] In the same way that he would have superiors pray for their religious and request prayers for themselves, so does he also insist that the simple prayer of the obedient person will have more efficacy than ten thousand uttered by one who is disobedient or uncompliant.[36]

4) ACCEPTING CORRECTION

Toward the end of his life Augustine was faced with a controversy concerning the nature of grace, a controversy which had broken out in a monastery not under his direction. Some of the monks of this monastery claimed that the superior should indeed prescribe what was to be done and pray for his religious that they might carry out their orders. But should they fail, the superior should not correct or rebuke them. This is a very interesting concept of obedience. And maybe it is not too far from some modern-day approaches which would make the superior little more than the "errand boy or girl" of the community. St. Augustine very deftly answers this problem by citing the practice of the Apostles. In effect, he says, they prescribed what was to be done, admonished if things were not properly done, and prayed that things would get done. Augustine applies their example to the practice of charity, that same charity which is the very purpose for which religious come together in community.

[The Apostle] gives orders so that charity be practiced; he
admonishes because charity is not practiced; he prays that charity
may abound. In the superior's commands, then, learn what you ought
to have; in his admonitions learn that it is by your own fault that this
is lacking to you; by his prayers learn the source from which you can
get what you wish to have.[37]

With this example in mind, we come back to what was said previously concerning Augustine's insistence on the obligation of the superior to correct those who are unruly, those who in any way infringe upon the harmony and unity of the religious house by ignoring or acting contrary to the *Rule* and the superior's commands. However, it would be well to add that Augustine is not asking submission of the mind to one's superiors; we do not have to agree with them. It is rather the will which he wants us to offer to God through religious obedience. A famous Augustinian theologian spelled out this idea over six centuries ago. What he said is well repeated here: *"No one is to be prevented from holding a contrary viewpoint when this can be done without danger to the faith . . . for our intellect is not a captive in submission to man, but in submission to Christ."*[38]   Nevertheless, no one will deny that submission of the will is a very difficult task.

Augustine was certainly right in stating that obedience is the virtue of the humble, the virtue of those who know their weakness, their sinfulness, who they really are.[39]   It is only the humble who can bear the burden of evangelical obedience or of evangelical authority in the likeness of Christ, who also humbled himself and became obedient even to dying for us.[40]

Bearing One Another's Burdens

Jean Vanier, founder of l'Arche, says that leaders in a community have a twofold mission:

> They must keep their eyes and those of the community fixed on what is essential, on the fundamental aims of the community . . . but their mission is also to create an atmosphere of mutual confidence, peace and joy among the community's members.[41]

While this is very true, perhaps we should also add that superiors cannot create such an atmosphere of confidence, peace and joy by themselves alone. They need the help of each and every member of the community, or they will fail. The religious must be prepared to bear the burdens of their superiors, and vice versa. They must not expect superiors to be without human failings any more than they themselves are. It would truly be very immature to propose to follow superiors and obey them, only as long as they remained without fault. This would be something like falling into the Donatist schism against which Augustine had to fight so long in his own day. As was quoted above: "*If you only obey those who are right, you obey no one.*"[42]

When we commit ourselves to following Christ, we pledge to follow him in the obscure light of faith, without the satisfaction that comes from certainty. This includes following him in good times and in bad, in good health and in ill, in times of growth and in times of failure. By professing obedience we do make a kind of leap into the unknown, for we cannot read the future with any clarity. But this leap is one of deep faith and trust in him who calls us. It is something like the practical response that Abraham gave to God when he was invited to leave family, home and friends. He set out, not knowing for sure just where he was going or when he would arrive, but confident in the overall concern and care of God for him.[43]   Both as superiors and as those who obey, we do the same. And that is why we need one another to reach the goal which has been placed before us.

9

LOVE THE LORD, LOVE THE CHURCH

ONE OF THE MOST DIVISIVE VOTES that was taken during the four years in which the Second Vatican Council was in session occurred on October 29, 1963. The vote did not concern any matter of faith or morals, or any important pastoral theme. What it did concern, however, was without doubt charged with theological overtones, although these were hidden behind a rather bland-sounding proposition. The matter in question was simply this: Was the Council's treatment of the Blessed Virgin Mary to be incorporated into the document on the Church, or was it to stand on its own as a separate document? Out of the almost 2200 votes cast that day, a margin of only 40 determined that the proper place to treat the Blessed Mother was not apart, but within the structure of the document on the Church.[1]

For those who know the mind of St. Augustine, this outcome of what had been a hotly debated subject would have seemed only logical. No one has higher words of praise for the Blessed Mother and for her unique role in the Lord's plan of salvation than Augustine. Yet at the same time, no one states more clearly that, despite her exalted role, Mary is still only a member of the Church: a very special member, it is true, but still only a member:

> Mary is holy, she is blessed, yet the Church is better than the Virgin Mary. Why? Because Mary is a part of the Church, a holy member, an excellent member, an outstanding member, but still a member of the whole body. If she is a part of the whole body, it is clear that the body is greater than its member.[2]

I do not use this example to introduce Augustine's teaching on the blessed Mother. Rather I use it because it seems to illustrate very concisely the overall importance for Augustine of the Church, that Church whose head is the Lord Jesus, and whose head and body together constitute the whole Christ. That we understand Augustine's great love and esteem for the Church right from the outset will help us appreciate even better his view of the place of religious in the Church, and what the Church can and should rightly expect of religious.

The *Rule* of St. Augustine says not a word about the Church, nor about the apostolate of religious in the Church. Yet this is not surprising: the *Rule* is very short, totally concerned with the internal life of the religious, making no attempt to address itself to other matters.[3] However, in some of his other writings Augustine does have some very clear and challenging ideas on religious in the Church. And that is what I would like to briefly synthesize in what follows.

Religious in the Church

Augustine began his own experience of the religious life with a very contemplative orientation. When he was ordained a priest, and then shortly afterwards a bishop, he had to alter this perspective radically, though he never lost his yearning for the contemplative lifestyle.[4]

The direct apostolate may have been literally forced upon Augustine through his unexpected ordination. But once he had accepted the burdens of the priesthood and the episcopacy, there was never any question about his responding generously to the pressing demands which these offices laid upon him. At the same time, however, his love of community, his contemplative orientation, and the innate restlessness which guided his search for God and the truth were to give a dynamic, new dimension to his priestly service. This new dimension, moreover, was soon to spread throughout the Church, perhaps principally because of the influence of Augustine's example. For with the founding of his first monastery in Hippo right after his priestly ordination, the priesthood and active ministry began to be joined to the religious life in the case of not a few of the brethren, and the basic contemplative thrust of the religious life began to be fused with the more active elements of the pastoral ministry.[5]

The first ones to be influenced by this combination of religious life and active ministry were the members of Augustine's own monastery in Hippo. Possidius, who was one of those more immediately influenced, gives us an idea of the chain reaction which was produced when members of Augustine's community took over other episcopal sees and established monasteries of their own:

> Those who served God in the monastery under the guidance of St.
> Augustine and together with him began to be ordained priests of the
> church of Hippo. . . . In fact, upon request, the blessed Augustine
> gave to various churches — some very important — about ten holy

and venerable, chaste and learned men, whom I myself knew. On the other hand, these men, who had come from their holy way of life to serve the churches of God scattered in various places, set about founding monasteries and . . . preparing brothers to receive the priesthood, who were themselves put in charge of other churches.[6]

Behind the fervor of this spiritual and cultural formation of the clergy for the Church in Africa, many of whom came from the ranks of Augustine's own religious, there lay a solid theology of the Church, to which Augustine gave expression on various occasions. This theology saw the religious life as being fundamentally at the service of the Gospel because of its unique place in the Church, which is the Mother of each and every member of the whole Christ.

Here is how he expressed these views when writing to the Abbot Eudoxius and his monks on the Isle of Capraria, a monastery which was not under Augustine's jurisdiction:

We exhort you in the Lord, brothers: persevere to the very end in the practice of the religious ideal you have embraced. Moreover, if the Church should request your services, do not accede to this request out of a desire to get ahead, nor refuse it moved by pleasureful idleness. Obey God, rather, in simplicity of heart, submitting yourselves humbly to him who directs you. . . . *Neither should you prefer your peaceful leisure to the needs of the Church: if there were no good people to minister to her as she gave birth, not even you would have found a way to have been born.*[7]

On a later occasion he expressed some parallel thoughts to Laetus, a young religious of his own monastery, who had returned home to settle some family affairs and who was now finding himself being torn from his vocation by an overprotective mother:

The Church, your mother, is also the mother of your mother. This Church conceived both of you through Christ . . . and gave you life so that you might attain eternal life. . . . This mother, scattered about the entire earth, is tormented by the assaults of error. . . . . She is also afflicted by the laziness and indifference of so many of the children she carries in her bosom, as well as by seeing so many of her members grow cold in various places, while she becomes less able to help her little ones. *Who then will give her the rightly necessary help she cries for, if not other sons and other members to whose number you belong?*[8]

Finally, in a well known text from *The City of God,* we can see how Augustine uses comparable ideas as he speaks in general about the three modes of life which are open to all people: the contemplative, the active, and the mixture of these two. He does not specifically mention the Church or service to the Church, but all that he says about the compelling nature of love fits in perfectly with what the two previous citations teach.

No one should be so given to leisure that in this condition he give no thought to his neighbor's needs; nor so given to activity that he allow no time for the contemplation of God. The attraction of leisure ought not to lie in a vacuous inactivity, but in the search for or the discovery of truth. . . . *Wherefore, the love of truth seeks out holy leisure, while the compelling force of love takes on necessary activity.* But if no one imposes this burden, time should be passed in searching out and looking into truth. *If, however, the burden is imposed, it ought to be borne because of the compelling force of love.* However, not even in this case should the attraction of truth be entirely abandoned, lest that delight be lost, and the burden crush him.[9]

Basic Principles for the Guidance of Religious in the Church

What can we gather from these and other expressions of Augustine's mind which concern religious and their apostolate in the Church? I believe we can draw the following conclusions or principles regarding Augustine's position:

1) Religious are expected to persevere in their vocation to the very end; nothing should make them abandon it. In other words, religious are primarily expected to be what

their vocation calls them to be in the Church: model Christians, the consecrated of God.[10]

2) If the Church does not call them, religious are to utilize their holy leisure or quiet time in search of the truth, in other words, in the prayerful contemplation of God. But at the same time, religious should be mindful that even this contemplation is a gift to be shared with others. What Augustine says to the laity in one of his sermons applies with even greater force to consecrated religious: *"Preach Christ wherever you can, to whomever you can and in whatever way you can. Faith is demanded of you, not eloquence.... The one who does not give to others is ungrateful to the one who has filled him. Therefore, in the manner in which each one has been filled, he is expected to give."*[11]

3) If the Church does call them, the compelling nature of love demands that religious shoulder any necessary sacrifices for the greater good of the Church, without, however, abandoning their fundamental religious vocation and dedication.

4) The Church relies particularly on those who have already been blessed with special graces by God to help her give birth to new sons and daughters and spread the Gospel. Augustine emphasizes forcefully the obligation of these people to serve others, because they have little or no need to attend to themselves: *"Those whom the Gospel and the grace of God have made perfect, live in this world only for the sake of others. They no longer need their life for themselves."*[12]

5) Finally, the service which may be requested of religious by the Church should not be taken on out of ambition, that is, out of a desire to move up in the world or in the Church itself, nor out of a desire for honor or personal advantage, but simply because "the love of Christ compels us."[13]

It is interesting that Augustine should speak explicitly of excluding ambition, honor and personal advantage even in the case of religious who undertake a special service to the Church. His own experience must have put him in contact with some clergy and/or religious who were ambitious and self-seeking. In any case he was sufficiently concerned by what he observed to bring it to the attention of others. He had just been ordained a priest when he wrote to his bishop Valerius in these words:

> In this life, and especially in these times, there is nothing easier, more pleasureful, more sought after than the office of bishop, or priest, or deacon, if these are going to be carried out lightly, amid the allurements of flatterers. But in the eyes of God, there is nothing more miserable, more regrettable, more worthy of condemnation. . . . On the other hand, provided this service is carried out as our Master commands, in the eyes of God there is no greater happiness.[14]

Later on he would preach strongly of the need for all the Church's shepherds to speak with only one voice, the one voice of Christ. For if they were to speak from schism or heresy or out of a search for personal advantage, they would only be feeding themselves, not their flock, and these would easily be confused and led astray.[15]

The main point that Augustine seems to be trying to make is this: no matter what position we may be in, we are at the service of the Church, because the Church is Christ, the whole Christ, and also our spiritual mother. All ministers must be united with her in carrying out their particular mission, because every true mission comes as a mandate from Christ through the Church.

> "If the Lord does not build the house, the builders labor in vain. . . ." Who are those who labor to build it? All those who in the Church preach the word of God, the ministers of God's sacraments. All of us run, all of us labor, all of us build. . . . But, "if the Lord does

not build the house, the builders labor in vain." . . . We speak from
without, he builds from within. . . . It is he who builds, counsels,
inspires fear, opens minds and directs them to the faith.[16]

Religious are not only very much a part of this reality of the
Church but, as Augustine puts it, a very honorable part, a model
part.[17]   In the same way that the members of the early
Jerusalem community were closely joined to the Apostles and
instructed by them,[18]   so also must religious today be closely
united to the Church and concerned principally about her needs,
not their own. In the same way, every apostolic work must be
intimately related to the Church's needs and reality, because
everything the Spirit gives us is at the service of the common
good.[19]

United in Love in a Truly Catholic Church

But the Church's needs cannot be viewed only under the
narrow focus of what is happening immediately around us. As
Augustine sees it, one of the very important aspects of the
Church is precisely its *universality.* Augustine was very sensitive
concerning this point: his vision was not limited to the narrow
confines of his own local Church but, as we have already seen, he
was more than willing to provide for the missionary needs of the
Church wherever these arose.[20]   Perhaps because of his per-
sistent problems with the Donatists, who indeed had a very
restricted view of the Church, Augustine's own view matched
his identification of the Church with the "whole Christ,"
scattered throughout the world:

We are the holy Church. But I have not said 'We' as though to
indicate only we who are here, you who have just been listening to
me. I mean all of us who are here and by the grace of God faithful
Christians in this church, that is, in this city; all those in this region,

in this province, across the sea, all those in the whole world. . . . Such
is the Catholic Church, our true mother, the true spouse of so great a
husband.[21]

There are near us, here in Africa, countless tribes of peoples, among
whom the Gospel has not yet been preached. . . . The Church,
therefore, must also be established in the midst of those people where
it is not yet present.[22]

It is this truly catholic, universal Church that we are called
to love, understand, sacrifice for, be joined to in unity, serve with
a generous heart, and bear up with when we find some bad
members mixed in with the many good. Augustine brings many
of these concepts together in a statement which challenges both
the committed apostle and the ordinary faithful:

The one who loves his brother puts up with everything for the sake of
unity, because fraternal love consists in the unity of love. Suppose an
evil person would offend you, or one whom you judge to be evil or
even only imagine to be so. *Would you, because of this, abandon so
many others who are good.*"[23]

We should not be led to believe that Augustine is here
principally pointing to those who are separated from the Church
as the evil ones. As he frequently indicated to his catechumens,
the greatest stumbling block to the faith does not usually come
from those who are outside communion with the Church, but
from those who are within the Church, those who claim to be
Christians while they are anything but![24]

Many call themselves Christians, but that they certainly are not!
They are not what their title signifies, neither in their life, their
morals, their faith, their hope, their charity.[25]

No wonder, then, that as a newly baptized Christian,
Augustine would admire so much those who were in positions of

apostolic leadership in the Church, for they not only had to put up with such false Christians, but also had to govern those who were in poor spiritual health:

> They must have patience with the vices of the people in order to heal them, and before they can calm the tempest, they must bear its brunt. In such circumstances it is very difficult to maintain an exemplary conduct and keep one's spirit perfectly calm.[26]

Honor Your Father, Honor Your Mother

Finally, Augustine brings out very forcefully the identity between union with the Holy Trinity and with the Church itself. If we truly love the Father, we will necessarily love his Church, which is the whole Christ. In the same way, we cannot be united with the Holy Spirit and be carrying out the Spirit's work if in any way we are separated from the reality of the universal Church. We cannot honor and love God as our Father without likewise honoring and loving the Church as our mother. These ideas are beautifully woven together by Augustine in the following quotations:

> How does anyone come to know that he has received the Holy Spirit? Let him question his own heart. If he loves his brother, the Spirit of God dwells in him. Let him put himself to the test before God: see if there is in him love for peace and unity, love for the Church spread thoughout the world.[27]

> We too, therefore, receive the Holy Spirit if we love the Church, if we are bound together by love, if we rejoice in the Catholic name and faith. Let us believe it, brothers and sisters: one will have the Holy Spirit in the same measure in which he or she loves the Church of Christ. . . . Moreover, we love the Church when we stand fast in her membership and love.[28]

But the most striking affirmation Augustine makes — which well demonstrates his own intense love of the Church

— puts the Church in such a close union with the Father that they are portrayed as being united in the marriage bond:

> Let us love the Lord our God, let us love his Church, him as our father, her as our mother; him as Lord, her as his servant, because we are sons and daughters of that servant. But this marriage is bonded together by the strongest love. No one can offend one and expect to be honored by the other. . . . What good will it do you not to offend the Father, if he will avenge the mother should she be offended? . . . Therefore, dearly beloved, let all with complete agreement cling to God as Father and to the Church as mother.[29]

Some Closing Reflections

It has always fascinated me to see how the Church has been central to the life of my own Augustinian Order since its foundation in the 13th century. For it was the Church herself, through two popes in particular, who gathered together various groups of religious in the year 1244 and again in 1256 to form our order. These various groups had been dedicated for the most part to the contemplative life, and yet the Church gave them at that time a very apostolic thrust, insisting at the same time that they not lose their contemplative dimension. The parallel with what happened to Augustine himself in coming from a very contemplative type of life to one that was surely both contemplative and active has never been lost on me.

I mention this because, just as there were inevitable tensions in Augustine's own life in seeking balance between the contemplative and the apostolic dimensions, so there are frequently such tensions in our own days among all religious who are sincerely striving to be what they are called to be in the Church.

Augustine addressed this problem in many different ways, but it practically always remained a problem for him. In his book *The City of God*, we have seen how he expected those called to

activity never to abandon the spiritual, interior joys of contemplation.[30]   Though very much involved in his apostolic
work for the people, he always made time in his daily round of
activities for the most important activity of all: his contemplative, interior, quiet prayer with God. He effectively taught his
fellow religious and the clergy associated with him that before
they could be real preachers of the Word, they had to be men of
prayer, drinking in the Word which God would give them,
before sharing it with others.[31]   He put into practice in his own
life what Pope John Paul II has underlined frequently in his talks
to religious around the world: *"A pause of true adoration has
greater value and spiritual advantage than the most intense activity,
even though it be apostolic activity."*[32]

Perhaps what this must bring us to ask ourselves is: How
are we facing this challenge in our own lives today? Unless a close
union exists between these two dimensions of our lives, unless
the contemplative dimension is really allowed to supply input
for our pastoral activity, there is a great danger of spiritual
sterility setting in, or of routine and even apathy making their
presence felt in our service to others. And if that were to happen,
I wonder if we could say that we were still being faithful to our
call within the Church to be model Christians.

A Broader Vision of the Church

Another point which Augustine's view of the Church
should inspire in all religious is this: Our vision of the Church
cannot be limited to our own backyard.

Augustine was dedicated to the Church: catholic and universal. He was open to the far-reaching needs of the entire body of
Christ, not tied down by the real problems he had to face in his
own diocese. His was a truly missionary view of the Church, and
he responded to this view in a very practical way, sending others
to help the Church where great need was apparent.

We can all be proud of the many contributions our respective religious congregations have made to the Church in the past. Even so, we must remain sensitive to the emerging, changing needs of the Church. We have to keep questioning ourselves as to how we can better respond to these needs as they develop, always taking into consideration, of course, our limitations, our distinctive charism, our very reason for existence in the Church. The more we are faithful to our call in the Church, the more we will be mission-minded, even though we may never leave home, just as happened in the case of St. Therese of Lisieux.

To love the Lord and love his Church — the "whole Christ" — is a joyful task, but also, and always, a challenging one. For those who wish to follow Augustine's spirit, it is also the way we minister to our spiritual Mother who has given us birth and continues to nourish us all. For it is precisely in this way that other sons and daughters will be able to receive the same grace accorded to us, and so be born and nourished in the Gospel.

10

BUILDING COMMUNITY
THROUGH TRUST
AND MUTUAL CONCERN

THE AUGUSTINIAN EXPERIENCE of community life presents an ideal that is both attractive and demanding.[1] It attempts to fuse the two distinct parts of this ideal into one: the spiritual, which has as its principal goal the common search for God; and the human, which is concerned with the building up of mutual relationships which will result in a loving, welcoming, supportive, challenging community. These two realities are able to be fused because, in keeping with Augustine's view, a growing awareness of the presence of God in one another inspires religious to realize their search for God first of all in the very heart of their community. It is in their mutual relationships, therefore, that the search for God finds its starting point and gains momentum. This search makes constant, concrete demands on each one, demands that can be summed up in one fundamental ideal: *each is to bear the burdens of the others as though these burdens were his or her own.* This is what constitutes the perfect fulfillment of the law of Christ: that we love one another as he loved us.

Such a way of life is neither unrealistic nor romantic. But it is truly a *way of life,* and as such, a life-long effort is necessary for the full achievement of its goals. The effort necessary for achieving that mutual love and concern, that harmony and concord which are so distinctive of Augustine's approach to community, is very aptly expressed in a sermon he gave on one occasion when the local Christian community was gathered for the dedication of a new church.

> This [church] is the house of our prayers, but we ourselves are the house of God. And if we ourselves are the house of God, we are being built up during our life here so that we may be dedicated at the end of time. A building, or rather the construction of that building, entails toil; the dedication, however, elicits only joy.
>
> What was done here while these walls were rising is reproduced when we bring together those who believe in Christ. . . . Nevertheless, they do not constitute a house of the Lord until they are joined together through love. If these beams and stones were not fitted together in a definite order, if they were not bound to one another in peace and, so to speak, united in love by mutual adhesion, no one would ever dare enter this house. But when you see a building in which the beams and stones are solidly joined together, you enter with confidence and have no fear that it will fall.[2]

The laying of the cornerstone of a church is a festive occasion, but it only marks the beginning of a great amount of strenuous labor on the part of many, so that the church may receive its exterior structure and attain its interior warmth. The same may be said for persons either entering the religious life or coming together to form a new community grouping — something that happens every time even one person is added to or taken away from the community. Much strenuous effort, many difficulties and disappointments lie ahead before the religious will learn how to form a true community of love in the Lord, before they will be able to reach that union with God, in and through their brothers or sisters, which is the ultimate goal Augustine proposes to those who wish to follow his religious ideal.

Many enter the religious life with unrealistic expectations. (It is quite possible that we ourselves may have had such unrealistic expectations at one time or another in the past.) They are not aware of their own limitations, nor of those of others. They frequently expect perfection and cannot find it. They seem oblivious to the fact that the religious life is 'life' itself, populated by human beings, not by angels. They are often very unprepared for the disappointments they will invariably meet because they do not find their ideals immediately realized. In synthesis, they do not realize that the building up of the community and of one's own vocation is a long, and sometimes quite tedious process.

Augustine's Earlier and Later Views of the
Religious Life

In his earliest days as a Christian, Augustine may well have had such a romantic understanding of the religious life, probably because he was viewing it as an outsider. This becomes evident, for example, from reading certain sections of his book *On the Customs of the Catholic Church*. In this particular work Augustine makes reference almost exclusively to what is positive in the religious life, a fact which could easily lead one to believe, quite falsely, that the religious life is a kind of paradise on earth. A brief passage from this work can serve as an example of this mentality:

Who can help but admire and commend those who, while disregard-
ing and setting aside the pleasures of this world and living together in
a truly chaste and holy society, unite in passing their time in prayers,
readings and discussions, without any swelling of pride, or noise of
contention, or sullenness of envy; but quiet, modest, peaceful, their
life is one of perfect harmony and devotion to God?[3]

The praise heaped upon the servants of God in this text
makes their life seem almost 'other-worldly,' far beyond the
capabilities of ordinary people. It would lead the reader to think
that these religious had already reached a kind of Nirvana or
state of perfection. Later, however, once Augustine had set
about leading the religious life himself, his views became both
very realistic and balanced. He saw the great amount of good
there is in this style of life, but at the same time, he did not
hesitate to underline also the many things that can go wrong in
living out this challenge.

This more realistic view becomes evident first of all in
Augustine's *Rule*, but also in other works. In these writings he
shows a remarkably balanced approach, insisting on the many
positive elements of community life, without, however, ignoring
the negative aspects which at times can also be found in the
monastery. He sees the religious life as a microcosm of the
Church itself, and in the Church there is always a mixture of
wheat and chaff among the members, be they laity, clergy or
religious.

My brothers and sisters, let no one deceive you. If you do not wish to
be deceived, and you want to love one another, then realize that every
state of life in the Church has its hypocrites. I did not say that every
person is a hypocrite, but rather that every state of life includes
people who are hypocrites. There are bad Christians just as there are
good ones.[4]

Any kind of life, if it is wrongly, that is, imprudently, recommended,
will attract people just because it is praised. But once these people

who have come to the monastery are inside, they find some whom
they had never imagined could be there. Fed up with the bad, they
also give up on the good.[5]

Even though good order reigns in my household, I am a man and I
live among men, nor would I dare to say that my home is better than
Noah's ark, where one of eight was cast out . . . nor better than the
community of the Lord Christ, in which eleven faithful souls put up
with the faithless thief Judas. . . . No, but I tell you in all simplicity
before the Lord our God, who is my witness . . . that with great
difficulty have I met persons better than those who have made
progress in the monastery. But at the same time neither have I met
worse than those who in the monastery have fallen from their
vocation.[6]

A Public Investigation

There is nothing like a practical case to illustrate the
difficulties that Augustine himself ran into in one of his own
monasteries, a case which severely tested his religious ideal in
the eyes of the entire local Church. What could have proved a
disaster was actually turned around to show the community and
the ideal in a very positive light, despite human weaknesses. In
his *Sermon 355* which he gave shortly before Christmas of the
year 425 — he was 71 years old at the time — we learn that he
was very upset because one of the priests who had been living
with him, a certain Januarius, had recently died and left a last will
and testament. This was strictly forbidden, because no one in his
monastery was to have any personal property or funds. As a
result of this, Augustine told the people he would conduct a
thorough investigation about how the other clerics in his community were living their vow of common life. When finally he
presented his conclusions to an overflowing crowd in church
some weeks later, he showed a justifiable pride: he had found
that all his brothers were loyal to their "holy commitment" to
live in common without having anything of their own.[7]   They

were, therefore, men after his own heart and a credit to the ideal
he had placed before them.

A Trusting Leader

The investigation had a happy ending. But a nagging
question remains to be answered: How did this problem arise in
the first place? Was it possible that Januarius could have lived for
years with Augustine and his community without any of them
having any cause for suspicion of wrongdoing? That, in fact,
seems to have been the case. Still, it is not difficult to understand
how this could have happened, if we bear in mind the basic
attitude that guided Augustine in his everyday dealings with his
fellow religious.

Augustine was very much aware of that fundamental truth
he constantly taught others, namely that each of us is a temple of
God. And this made him a very trusting person. He thought too
much of his brothers to be suspicious of their private lives. It is
evident that he considered this attitude of trust just as essential
for the overall harmony of the community as his insistence, for
example, on a total sharing of goods in the monastery. The
mutual respect which all the brothers were to have for one
another was intended to exclude from their common life that
grave disturbance which invariably results when suspicions are
allowed to take root, grow and eventually poison fraternal relationships. This attitude of respect and trust is especially important for one who is placed at the head of the community, and
whose principal task in the Augustinian framework is not to
delve into the secrets of others' consciences, but to protect and
promote unity and harmony in the community. What that unity
and harmony meant to Augustine has already been indicated.[8]
He expressed his mind on this matter of trust very clearly when
he addressed the faithful concerning the case of Januarius:

I have such a good opinion of my brethren that I have refrained from asking them questions, because it seemed to me that in questioning them I might almost appear to suspect some evil. On the other hand, I was aware then as now that all those who have lived with me are familiar with our ideal and rule of life.[9]

This same element of trust shows up in the *Rule* when Augustine speaks of the care of the sick:

If the cause of a brother's bodily pain is not apparent, you must take the word of God's servant when he indicates what is giving him pain.[10]

Possidius gives us other insights into this trust, which touch on the very delicate area of finances:

He delegated and entrusted alternately to the more able clerics the administration and all the goods of the house connected to the church. For himself he kept neither key nor signet ring. Those who were put in charge recorded all the income and debits. At the end of every year an accounting was made to him, so that he could know how much had been received and distributed or what remained to be distributed. But in many transactions he trusted the administrator rather than verify the precisely documented figures.[11]

Augustine was even willing to apply this same trusting attitude toward those who aspired to enter the monastery, a fact which constitutes just one more example of his extraordinary openness and understanding of human psychology. Let them prove themselves, he says to a hypothetical superior, pointing out how difficult it is to judge others without having some personal experience of them.

How will you get to know the one you want to exclude from the monastery? If you want to find out that he is unfit, you must put him to the test, and this must be done in the monastery itself.... Will you refuse to accept all the unfit? That's what you say.... But will they all

present themselves to you with their hearts in their hands? Some
postulants do not even know themselves; how much less will you
know them? Many have promised themselves that they will generously respond to the holiness of that life which possesses all things in
common, where no one claims anything as his own, and they are of
one mind and heart intent upon God. They have been put in the fire
and they have crumbled.[12]

Through these few examples it becomes sufficiently clear
that Augustine observed an attitude of fundamental trust toward
those who lived with him. At the same time, however, he
demanded much of them. He expected of them a very mature
approach to their commitment of living together in harmony in a
common search for God. This maturity and sense of responsibility are at the very heart of his *Rule*, which continually calls
individuals to be honest with themselves and with the community, as those who are no longer slaves, but living in freedom
under grace.

Suspicion, no! — Responsibility, yes!

Avoiding a suspicious nature, however, is not to be confused with adopting a "laissez faire" attitude to those in the
community. In the face of clear signs of failings, wrongdoing or
attitudes which imperil the community or the vocation of an
individual, one has to act just as Augustine did. He never turned
a blind eye in the face of evident disorders. Possidius, for
example, tells us how Augustine reacted strongly when some
fellow-bishops, who were eating at his table, began to talk about
some brothers who were absent. He immediately showed his
displeasure and reproached them sharply.[13]   Why did he react
so quickly and strongly? Because the offense was blatant and
went against the most fundamental principles of community
living.

Yet most corrections will not be of this nature. Probably
most situations in community life demand an entirely different

approach, one that seeks to protect the good name of the individual when matters have not reached the point of public scandal.[14]   It is one thing, therefore, to be trusting and avoid undue suspicion. It is quite another thing to be concerned about the good health of the community — that is, of the individuals who make it up — so that expedient action may be taken when necessary. Superiors who allow things to deteriorate to such a degree that a cure becomes useless or practically impossible do as much harm to the community as those who, without sufficient foundation, adopt a suspicious attitude toward their religious. But what is true of superiors is also true of every member of the community. Persons who go around "looking for trouble" are of no help to the unity and harmony of the community, any more than those who never want to get involved in the nitty-gritty of community building. Mutual trust and respect, which arise from mutual concern and love, and which show themselves in practical ways, are essential to unity and harmony in the community.

Even though at times mistakes may be made in allowing some people to enter religious life, and some may later discover they had no real vocation, or may go back on the vocation they once freely accepted, Augustine nevertheless believed that *"our holy fraternity is not endangered because of those who profess to be what they are not."*[15]   Such people, he says, *"cannot easily be sent away unless they have first been put up with."*[16]   Here again we are reminded of Augustine's idea that we serve, honor and worship God in and through our fellow religious *by bearing one another's burdens.* As Augustine sees it, we have to put up with the trying problems caused by some unfit or hypocritical religious, for the sake of the many good ones. By our joyful perseverance in the face of trial, we lend support to the vocation of those many others, indeed the vast majority, who are striving to lead a good religious life.[17]

In the same vein, as Augustine points out elsewhere, Jesus did not come to save us when we were free from sin, but precisely because we were burdened with sin. On the other hand, however, Jesus did not come so that we would remain sinners, but so that we might grow and become what we were not yet.[18] Fundamentally this must also be our attitude in the religious life. We must ask from God the gift to love one another as Jesus loved us. For quite frankly we will only really love one another when we love God in the other *"either because God lives in that person already or so that God may come to live in him. . . ."*[19] Nevertheless, such an attitude of love and basic trust does not prevent us from taking firm steps to safeguard the unity and harmony of the community when other, milder attempts have repeatedly failed. *"This is not done out of cruelty"*, writes Augustine, *"but from a sense of compassion so that many others may not be lost through the bad example"* of one or another.[20]

Deeper Respect and Sensitivity

Some practical consequences for living in community can be drawn from these reflections. As we emerge from an era which was often characterized by mistrust and lack of confidence, we are being called to acquire a deeper respect for one another as persons, sons and daughters of God with a common calling. This respect for others will be born, first of all, from our own self-respect, that is, from an understanding of who we are and what God is trying to effect in, through and for us. This should lead us to appreciate better how God is working to the same purpose in others, despite the inevitable obstacle which our common human nature throws up against his grace.

Putting the matter into everyday human terms, it means that we should be led to a greater sensitivity toward others: toward their needs, hopes and anxieties, their loneliness and their joyful moments, their desire to be listened to and to be understood. We cannot hope to accompany the others physically at prayer, work and recreation, while remaining detached from their feelings and concerns. To achieve this, however, many still have to learn to let go of the hurts of the past, which can effectively keep them from growing and changing for the better. We all have to learn anew to listen to one another in the new environment which has been created throughout the religious life since Vatican II and the renewal of our Constitutions.

There is very little unity in a pile of bricks, placed side by side, even though they touch or rub against one another. Unity only results when they are bound together in a meaningful and stable way. The same is true of religious communities. We cannot simply live in them, side by side. We must give them substance and meaning by being firmly joined together through love, trust, mutual concern and support. Those who are stronger will be asked to give greater support; those who are quicker will know that they are called to encourage others to stay in the race and keep moving ahead; those who are more talented may perhaps effectively contribute more to the building up of the community, but never by pushing their fellow religious into the shadows. Augustine offers some very meaningful advice concerning the practicalities of such an effort, which involves example, challenge and encouragement.

> We know we are travelling together. If our pace is slow, go on ahead of us. We won't envy you, but rather will seek to catch up with you. But if you consider us capable of a quicker pace, then run along with us. There is only one goal and we are all anxious to reach it, some at a slow pace, and others more quickly.[21]

> If some are quicker than others in understanding, let them reflect that they are walking along the road together with those who are slower. When two companions take the same road, and one is faster than the other, it is in the power of the faster to allow the slower one to catch up, not vice versa. In fact, if the faster walks with all the speed he is capable of, the slower brother will not succeed in following. It is necessary, therefore, that the one who is faster slow his pace so as not to abandon his slower companion.[22]

In these passage we are reminded of what St. Paul wrote, namely, that we all have different gifts according to the special grace that has been given each one, but all these gifts are at the service of the community.[23]   Again and again Augustine makes the point that our commitment to God is to be realized in a practical way through our commitment to one another. Even the quick and the strong have their moments of hesitation and weakness. We all need one another's support in living out the vocation to which we have been called. We all need to bear one another's burdens if we are going to form a real community. And when we do this out of love, with that respect and trust which come from acknowledging the presence of God in our brothers and sisters, then, difficulties notwithstanding, unity and harmony, which constitute the holy commitment of the community on its way to God, will flourish, and we will know that interior peace which God alone can grant to those who love him in his little ones.[24]

ENDNOTES

CHAPTER 1: *Community Life: The Augustinian Experience*

1 See *Confession* 4, 4, 7. Unless otherwise specified, all quotations from the *Confessions* of St. Augustine are taken from the translation of John K. Ryan, Garden City, N.Y.: Image Books, 1960. For a further development of this idea see also above, Ch. 3, "True Friends in Christ."

2 Ibid., 6, 14, 24.

3 Ibid., 8, 6, 14.

4 Ibid., 8, 8-12.

5 Ibid., 9, 4-6.

6 *De moribus ecclesiae catholicae* I, 31-33. (Hereafter: *De mor. eccl. cath.*)

7 Possidius, *The Life of Augustine*, 3, 1, hereafter referred to simply as "Possidius." An English translation of this *Life* may be found in E.A. Foran, O.S.A., *The Augustinians*. London: Burns Oates & Washbourne, 1938. All citations in this book are the author's translation.

8 That is, the Jerusalem community: see Ac 4:32-35. (All Scripture quotes are taken from *The New American Bible*, copyright 1970 and 1986 by the Confraternity of Christian Doctrine, Washington, D.C.)

9 Possidius, 5, 1: also *Sermon* 355, 2.

10 *The Rule of Saint Augustine*, with Introduction and Commentary by T.J. van Bavel, O.S.A., Tr. by R. Canning, O.S.A., London: Darton, Longman and Todd, 1984, pp. 3-4.

11 *Sermon* 355, 2.

12 *Sermon* 356, 2.

13 *The Rule of St. Augustine*, no. 3 (ch. 1, 2). Unless otherwise specified, all quotations from the *Rule* are taken from the translation of Robert P. Russell, O.S.A., Villanova, PA: Province of St. Thomas, 1976. Fr. Russell uses a continuous numbering of the paragraphs of the *Rule*. The reference given in parentheses (ch. 1, 2) refers to van Bavel's translation.

14 Ibid., no. 9 (ch. 1, 8); see also *En. in Ps.* 131, 5.

15 *Letter* 243, 4.

16 Tarcisius van Bavel, O.S.A., "Community Life in Augustine," *The Tagastan* [now known as *Augustinian Heritage*] 29 (1983) no. 2, p. 124. See also the *Code of Canon Law*, 607, 1 where the accent is put on personal consecration. The total existence of the religious is thus a continuous act of worship toward God in charity.

17 See *Rule*, no. 8 (ch. 1, 7).

18 Jn 17:21.

19 *Rule*, no. 31 (ch. 5, 2).

20 Mt 25:31-46; St. Augustine, *Sermon* 389, 4-5; *Sermon* 60, 8-10.

21 *Rule*, nos. 4-9 (ch. 1, 3-8); no. 32 (ch. 5, 3).

22 Ibid., nos. 10-13 (ch. 2, 1-4).

23 Ibid., nos. 14-17 (ch. 3, 1-4).

24 Ibid., no. 18 (ch. 3, 5); no. 37 (ch. 5, 8).

25 Ibid., no. 24 (ch. 4, 6).

26 Ibid., nos. 25-26 and 28 (ch. 4, 7-8 and 10).

27 Ibid., no. 31 (ch. 5, 2).

28 Ibid., no. 36 (ch. 5, 7).

29 Ibid., nos. 41-42 (ch. 6, 1-2).

30 Ibid., nos. 44-47 (ch. 7, 1-4).

31 *En. in Ps.* 132, 9.

32 Adolar Zumkeller, O.S.A. *Augustine's Ideal of the Religious Life*. Tr. by E. Colledge. Fordham University Press: New York, 1986, pp. 126-127.

33 T. van Bavel, O.S.A. "Espiritualidad Agustiniana," in *Presencia*, La Paz, Bolivia, domingo 16 nov. 1980. See also T. van Bavel, O.S.A., "Community Life in Augustine," *The Tagastan* 29 (1983) no. 2, pp. 128-129: "[In Egyptian monasticism] we find at the head of the community an abba or amma, through whom the younger monks listen to the voice of the Holy Spirit. . . With [Augustine] it is rather the whole community that is gathered around the Gospel and is listening to Christ as our inner Master. Consequently, the building up of the community is considered much more as a task for every member of the group. We have to listen to Christ and his message as a group."

34 A. Manrique - A. Salas, O.S.A. *Evangelio y Comunidad*. Ed. "Biblia y Fe." Escuela Biblica: Madrid, 1978, pp. 201-202. See also: L. Verheijen, O.S.A., "Acts 4, 31-35 in the Monastic Texts of St. Augustine," in *Second Annual Course on Augustinian Spirituality*. Rome: 1976, p. 58: "St. Augustine realized that this fraternity in a monastery is a concrete form of the brotherly spirit of the whole Church; the *anima una* is the *anima unica Christi*."

35 "In the very things that somehow I know, I would rather find you well instructed than discover that you are in need of me. For we should not wish others to be ignorant so that we have something to teach them; it is better if we are all disciples of God. . . . Take it for absolutely certain that even if you can learn from me something good, your true Master will always be the interior Master of the interior man. . . ." St. Augustine, *Letter* 266 to Florentina, cited in L. Verheijen, O.S.A. *Saint Augustine: Monk, Priest, Bishop*. Villanova, PA: Augustinian Historical Institute, 1978, pp. 59-60. (Hereafter referred to as: *St. Augustine* . . .).

36 See St. Augustine, *En. in Ps.* 99, 12; *En. in Ps.* 75, 16; *Sermon* 355, 1. 1; also, A Manrique, *Teología Agustiniana de la Vida Religiosa*. El Escorial: Real Monasterio, 1964, P. II, c. 1, 115-124 (hereafter referred to as: *Teología*. . .).

CHAPTER 2: *Let Everything Be Yours In Common*

1 Pope Paul VI once remarked that the common life was not to be considered as just another aid for Augustinians in living the religious life. Rather it was to be looked upon as the goal towards which they would daily strive, a veritable school of love. By equating the common life with the goal of love, the Pope was pointing out that the Augustinian ideal looks to find Jesus at the very center of the community, present in each and every one of the religious, as well as in all together. (Pope Paul VI, Address to the Augustinian General Chapter of 1971, in *Living in Freedom Under Grace*. Rome: Curia Generalizia Agostiniana, 1979, p. 42. Hereafter referred to as *Living in Freedom*.)

2 Augustine, *En in Ps*. 131, 5.

3 *Rule*, no. 4 (ch. 1, 3).

4 *Sermon* 355, 6.

5 *"Those people put their personal goods in common. Did they lose what had been their own? If they had kept for themselves what was their own, then each one would have only what was his own. But since he put in common what was his own, even what the others had became his"* (*En. in Ps*. 131, 5). This observation is reminiscent, on a more spiritual plane, of what Augustine wrote to Laetus, a religious who had left the monastery, presumably to take care of financial matters at home and then return. However, he was being impeded from returning by his mother's overpowering possessiveness. Augustine wrote to the young man, reminding him, among other things, that he no longer belonged only to himself, but also to his brothers in religion: *"Your soul does not belong to you alone; it belongs to all the brothers. And their souls belong to you. Or better, their souls, together with yours, are not many souls, but only one, the one soul of Christ"* (*Letter* 243, 4).

6 *Sermon* 355, 1. 2.

7 *Sermon* 356, 13.

8 *Rule*, no. 5 (ch. 1,4).

9 Ibid., no. 6 (ch. 1, 5).

10 Ibid., nos 38, 40 (ch. 5, 9, 11).

11 Ibid., no. 48 (ch. 8, 1).

12 *Letter* 157, 39; see also *En. in Ps*. 103, s. 3, 16.

13 *Sermon* 356, 9.

14 *Ac* 4:35.

15 *Rule*, nos. 14, 18 (ch. 3, 1, 5).

16 Ibid., nos. 16, 17 (ch. 3, 3-4).

17 Ibid., no. 30 (ch. 5, 1).

18 *En. in Ps*. 131, 26.

19 *En. in Ps*. 73, 24.

20 *En. in Ps*. 71, 3.

21 *Rule*, no. 19 (ch. 4, 1).

22 Possidius, 22; see also Augustine, *Letter* 48, 3.

23 *De opere monachorum* 25, 33. (Hereafter: *De op.mon.*)

24 Ph 2:7; 2 Cor 8:9.

25 Op. cit., no 23.
26 Ibid., no 24.
27 See, e.gr., Possidius, nos. 19-20.
28 Mt 4:4.
29 David M. Stanley, S.J. *Faith and Religious Life*. N.Y.: Paulist Press, 1971, pp. 83-84.
30 *Letter* 127, 6.
31 *Sermon* 345, 6, as cited in Boniface Ramsey, O.P., "The Center of Religious Poverty," in *Review for Religious* 42 (1983) no. 4, p. 539.
32 Boniface Ramsey, O.P., op. cit., pp. 534-544, but especially pp. 542-543.
33 See above, note 29.
34 Ac 5:1-11.
35 Cited in A. Sage, A.A. "La Contemplation dans les communautes de vie fraternelle," in *Recherches Augustiniennes* VII (1971) 283.
36 See above, note 5: *Letter* 243, 4.

CHAPTER 3: *True Friends In Christ*

1 With regard to all this, see, for example: Adolphe Tanquerey, *The Spiritual Life*. Westminster, MD: Newman Press, 1930, pp. 285-291. A good example of a spiritual or supernatural friendship would be that between St. Francis de Sales and St. Jane Frances de Chantal.
2 See *P.C.*, 2. (All quotations from the Second Vatican Council in this book are taken from: *The Documents of Vatican II*, edited by Walter M. Abbot, S.J. New York: Guild Press, 1966).
3 Sermon 299 D, 1; *Letter* 130, 6, 13.
4 See, for example, *Conf.*, 2, 5, 10; 4, 8, 13; 4, 9, 14; 6, 16, 26; *Letter* 73, 3; etc.
5 *Conf.* 4, 4, 7.
6 Possidius, 3; *Sermon* 355, 1. 2.
7 Marie Aquinas McNamara, O.P., *Friends and Friendship for St. Augustine*. Staten Island: Alba House, 1964, pp. 129, 133, 137, 142. See also: Teófilo Viñas, O.S.A., *La Amistad en la Vida Religiosa*. Madrid: Inst. Teológica de Vida Religiosa, 1982, pp. 173ff.
8 M.A. McNamara, pp. 144-211.
9 *Retractationes* I, 22; 25; *De libero arbitrio*; also the dialogues at Cassiciacum.
10 Jn 15:12-14.
11 Jn 15:13.
12 Jn 15:15.
13 e.gr., Job, passim; Ps 41:9; Ps 55:13; Pr 17:17; 18:24; 27:6.
14 There were, for example, some excesses involved in certain sensitivity sessions, or in an exggerated sentimentalism, which may have made the notion of friendship unwelcome for some. There have always been those few, especially among superiors, who, even without realizing it, have played favorites with their friends and effectively divided their communities as a result.
15 *Conf.* 4, 4, 7.
16 *Contra duas epistolas Pelagianorum* I, 1.

17 *Letter* 258, 4; see also *Conf.* 4, 9, 14: "Blessed is the man who loves you [Lord], and his friend in you, and his enemy for your sake. For he alone loses no dear one to whom all are dear in him who is not lost."

18 M.A. McNamara, p. 221.

19 *Conf.* 6, 16, 26; also T. van Bavel, O.S.A. *Christians in the World.* New York: Catholic Book Publishing Co., 1980, p. 25 (hereafter: *Christians.* . .).

20 *Sermon* 299 D, 1.

21 Ibid.

22 *Letter* 130, 2, 4.

23 Ibid.

24 *De civitate Dei* 19, 8 (hereafter: *De civ. Dei*). See above, note 13, for the same fears in Scripture.

25 *Letter* 28, 1, 1; see also *Conf.* 4, 8, 13; 2, 5, 10.

26 *Letter* 155, 1, 1.

27 *De diversis quaestionibus 83,* q. 71, 2 (hereafter: *De div. quaest.*).

28 Ibid., q. 71, 5.

29 Ibid., q. 71, 3.

30 Ibid., q. 71, 6.

31 Ibid., q. 71, 6: "We can consider that person to have been accepted by us as a friend with whom we have the courage to share even our inmost thoughts."

32 *Letter* 73, 3, 10.

33 *Letter* 68, 2, from Jerome to Augustine.

34 *Letter* 73, 2, 4.

35 *Letter* 155, 1, 1; 3, 11.

36 *Letter* 73, 2, 3-4.

37 T. van Bavel, *Christians* . . . pp. 26, 29.

38 *Letter* 130, 6, 13.

39 "He loves his friend truly who loves God in him, either because God is already in him or in order that he may be in him." *Sermon* 361, 1; see also *Commentary on 1 Jn 10:7.*

40 See above, chapter 1: "Community Life: the Augustinian Experience," pp. 7-8."

41 See above, p. 37.

42 *En. in Ps.* 132, 6.

43 *Letter* 243, 4: "Their souls, together with yours, are not many souls, but only one, the one soul of Christ."

44 *Rule* no. 3 (ch. 1, 2).

45 For these ideas concerning friendship in the *Rule*, see T. Aparicio, especially pp. 236-244.

46 *De div. quaest.*, q. 71, 5.

47 *Constitutions of the Order of St. Augustine,* Rome, 1978, nos. 27, 30, 31 (hereafter: *Const. O.S.A.*).

48 See above, notes 20, 24.

49 *Letter* 73, 3, 10.

CHAPTER 4: *Searching For God: Contemplation And The Interior Life*

1 *Conf.* 1, 1, 1.
2 Ibid., 3, 1, 1 (my translation).
3 Ibid., 5, 2, 2.
4 Ibid., 10, 27, 38; see also *Conf.* 6, 1, 1.
5 Ibid., 10, 8, 15.
6 Ibid., 10, 4, 6.
7 Ibid., 3, 6, 11.
8 *En. in Ps.* 41, 8. (Translation as in M. Pellegrino, *Give What You Command.* New York: Catholic Book Publishing Co., 1975.)
9 *De op. mon.* 29, 37; *Conf.* 10, 40, 65; 10, 43, 70.
10 *De vera religione* 39, 72.
11 *En. in Ps.* 33, sermon 2, 8 (as translated in M. Pellegrino, op. cit.).
12 *En. in Ps.* 76, 13-14 (as translated in M. Pellegrino, op. cit.).
13 *Conf.*, 7, 10, 16.
14 *Sermon* 261, 7.
15 *In ev. Io.*, tr. 20, 3.
16 *In 1 ep. Io.* 3, 13; see also *Sermon* 134, 1, 1.
17 *Sermon* 102, 2.
18 *Sermon* 52, 22; see also *En. in Ps.* 76, 8.
19 *De quantitate animae* 33, 74.
20 *Contra Faustum* 22, 52. See *Quaest. in Exod.* 68: "A soul which is too concerned with human affairs is in a sense emptied of God; on the other hand, the freer the soul is to rise up to heavenly and eternal things, the more it is filled with God." See also A. Trapè, O.S.A., "The Search for God and Contemplation," in *Searching for God.* Rome: Augustinian Publications, 1981, pp. 17-21.
21 "La Contemplation dans les communautes de vie fraternelle," in *Recherches Augustiniennes* VII (1971) 301.
22 See above, chapter 1: "Community Life: The Augustinian Experience."
23 *In 1 ep. Io.*, 5, 7; see also 9, 10; *De Trinitate* 8, 12.
24 *In ev. Io.*, tr. 17, 8.
25 *Sermon* 235, 3.
26 Verheijen, *St. Augustine. . .*, pp. 70-71.
27 *De civ. Dei* 19, 19.
28 Verheijen, *St. Augustine. . .*, pp. 22-23.
29 Mt 25:31-46.
30 *Sermon* 330, 3.
31 *In ev. Io.*, tr. 32, 4.
32 *Conf.* 11, 2, 3 (my translation).
33 *Soliloquia* I, 12, 20; 13, 22.
34 *In ev. Io.*, tr. 97, 1.
35 *In ev. Io.*, tr. 26, 7.

36 *En. in Ps.* 41, 9-10; the entire commentary on Psalm 41, especially from 8-10, is an ode to the joys of contemplation. See also, *Conf.* 10, 40, 65.

37 *In ev. Io.*, tr. 63, 1. This same text goes on to say: "Let us never cease to move forward along this way, until it brings us to where we can remain. . . . Seeking and finding we shall come to the goal, and there finally our search will end, where we shall have met with the perfection we seek."

38 *De Trinitate* 15, 2.

39 *Letter* 48; also Verheijen, *St. Augustine. . .*, pp. 23-24, 26-27.

40 *The Cloud of Unknowing*, ed. by Wm. Johnston. Garden City, N.Y.: Image Books, 1973. Ch. 34, p. 90; Ch. 39, p. 98.

41 *Conf.* 10, 27, 38.

CHAPTER 5: *Sign of Contradiction*

1 *Conf.* 8, 7, 17.

2 Ibid., 8, 5, 10.

3 Ibid., 2, 3, 5.

4 Ibid., 2, 2, 2.

5 *Sermon* 57, 9.

6 *Sermon* 151, 5.

7 *Conf.* 10, 30, 41.

8 *P.C.* 12.

9 *L.G.* 42; *O.T.* 10; *P.C.* 12.

10 A. Manrique, *Teología. . .*, P. II, c. 1, pp. 115-124. See also R.E. Heslinga, ed. *One Mind, One Heart* (private publication and translation of some parts of Manrique.) 1973, pp. 102-105.

11 *En. in Ps.* 75, 16; see also *De sacra virginitate* 8, 8. (Hereafter: *De s. virg.*)

12 *P.C.* 12; see also D.M. Stanley, op. cit., pp. 74-75.

13 *P.C.* 12.

14 For a fine presentation of the subject of intimacy in the religious life, see R.J. McAllister, M.D., *Living The Vows.* San Francisco: Harper & Row, 1986, especially pp. 38-51. For example: "The desire for intimacy should motivate a person to give of self in search of another, not to take from another in search of self" (p. 41).

15 Mt 19:11.

16 *Conf.* 6, 11, 20.

17 Ibid., 2, 7, 15; see also 8, 11, 27.

18 Ibid., 8, 17, 17.

19 *De s. virg.* 8, 8; see also *En. in Ps.* 99, 13.

20 *In. ev. Io.*, tr. 13, 12.

21 *De s. virg.* 11, 11.

22 *Sermon* 72 A, 7 (also knonwn as *Denis* 25, 7).

23 *De s. virg.* 3, 3.

24 *De civ. Dei* 10, 6.

25 Jn 15:12-15.
26 John M. Lozano, C.M.P. "Trends in Religious Life Today," in *Review for Religious*. 42 (1983) no. 4, p. 500.
27 1 Cor 7:32-34.
28 *Conf.* 10, 29, 40 (my translation).
29 Ibid., 10, 37, 61.
30 *Sermon* 161, 11, 11.
31 *De s. virg.* 51, 52.
32 *Sermon*, 57, 9.
33 *Sermon* 344, 1.
34 2 Cor 12:9-10.
35 See above, note 27.
36 *Rule*, no. 24 (ch. 4, 6).
37 Ibid., nos 25-28 (ch. 4, 7-10).
38 Ibid., nos. 20, 36 (ch. 4, 2; ch. 5, 7).
39 Ibid., nos. 10-14, and passim (ch. 2, 1-4; ch. 3, 1).
40 Ibid., no. 23 (ch. 4, 5).
41 Ibid., nos. 19, 21 (ch. 4, 1, 3).
42 Ibid., no. 22 (ch. 4, 2).
43 1 Cor 10:12.
44 Lk 18:9-14.
45 *De s. virg.* 34, 34.
46 Ibid., 41, 42.
47 See Jn 12:24.
48 Ep 1:4.
49 Lk 1:29-37.
50 *De s. virg.* 52, 53.

CHAPTER 6: *The Committed Christian and the Cross*

1 *L.G.* 40.   2 See *A.G.* 2; 4; 6 and passim.
3 *A.A.* 3, and passim.
4 *P.C.* 2a
5 *L.G.* 46.
6 *Rule*, no. 3 (ch. 1, 2): the unity proposed by Augustine would never be possible without such a 'radical' Christian outlook.
7 *Sermon* 128, 11; see also *Conf.* 10, 30, 42; 10, 31-37, concerning various of the temptations Augustine still was undergoing in his middle age.
8 Jn 15:13-14.

9 See Augustine, *En. in Ps.* 54, 10: "When you have looked with all sincerity on what he [Christ] has suffered, will you not also be able to bear your sufferings calmly, and maybe even joyfully, because you have found yourself in a similar way in the sufferings of your king?"

10 Jn 12:24.

11 Mt 13:44-46.

12 Mt 16:24.

13 Jn 12:25-26.

14 Jn 13:34-35.

15 Augustine: *De civ. Dei* 14, 28, as translated in van Bavel, *Christians...*, p. 61.

16 Gal 5:22-24.

17 See for all this: van Bavel, *Christians...*, pp. 38, 46; Rene Voillaume, *Spirituality from the Desert*, pp. 74-75; Giovanni Scanavino, O.S.A., "Lo Spirito di Penitenza," in *Bollettino di S. Rita*. Milano: April 1983, pp. 6-7.

18 Augustine: *Sermon* 96, 2, 2.

19 James Carroll "Mortification for Liberation," in *The National Catholic Reporter*, Advent 1971, as quoted in Martin W. Pable, O.F.M. Cap., "Psychology and the Commitment to Celibacy," in *Review for Religious* 34 (1975) no. 2, March.

20 *En. in Ps.* 36, sermon 2, 16.

21 *De mor. eccl. cath.* I, 33, 71 & 73.

22 Ibid.

23 *Rule*, no. 31 (ch. 5, 2).

24 *Sermon* 96, 7, 9.

25 *Sermon* 96, 4, 4.

26 *Sermon* 96, 7, 9.

27 *Letter* 243, 11.

28 *In ev. Io.*, 51, 12: "They serve Jesus Christ who do not seek their own interests, but those of Jesus Christ. 'Follow me', therefore, means: follow my ways, not your own...".

29 *De div. quaest. 83*, q. 71, 7.

30 *Const. O.S.A.*, no. 36.

31 *Sermon* 156, 9, 9.

32 *Conf.* 10, 31, 47; see also *En. in Ps.* 99, 11; Sermon 339, 1, where he speaks of the problem he experienced from being praised.

33 *Const. O.S.A.*, no. 38.

34 *Letter* 130, 16, 31.

35 *Sermon* 56, 8, 12; *Sermon* 58, 8, 10.

36 *Se utilitate ieiunii* 5, 6-7.

37 *Rule*, no. 14 (ch. 3, 1).

38 *De doctrina christiana* 1, 24-45.

39 *Const. O.S.A.*, no. 38, citing Bl. Simon of Cascia in the footnote.

40 *Rule*, no. 14 (ch. 3, 1).

41 *Rule*, no. 18 (ch. 3, 5).

42 *Rule*, nos. 19, 21 (ch. 4, 1; 3).

43 Ibid., no. 22 (ch. 4, 4).

44 Ibid., nos. 25-26 (ch. 4, 7-8).
45 Ibid., no. 32 (ch. 5, 3).
46 Ibid., no. 42 (ch. 6, 2).
47 Ibid., no. 49 (ch. 8, 2).
48 *Letter* 48, 3.
49 Op. cit., 22, 2-3, 5-6; 25, 2.
50 Ibid., 31, 1-2.
51 *De bono viduitatis* 21, 26.
52 *In ep. Io.*, 2, 14.

CHAPTER 7: *Clothe Yourselves With Humility*

1 Gospels, passim, especially John.
2 Mk 8:35.
3 Mt 19:30.
4 Lk 14:11.
5 Lk 1:52-53.
6 2 Cor 12:9-10.
7 1 Cor 1:18, 23-24, 27.
8 *Conf.* 2, 3, 7.
9 *Conf.* 3, 5.
10 Ibid., 5, 14, 24.
11 Possidius, 9-12.
12 *Tr. in Io. ev.* 25, 16; see also *Sermon* 117, 17.
13 *Sermon* 142, 2 (also known as *Wilmart* 11, 2).
14 *En. in Ps.* 93, 16.
15 *En. in Ps.* 38, 12, 18.
16 *Sermon* 123, 1 & 3; *En. in Ps.* 93, 15.
17 *Sermon* 123, 1; *Sermon* 354, 5.
18 Mt 9:12-13.
19 *En. in Ps.* 130, 12.
20 *Sermon* 137, 4; see also *Tr. in Io. ev.* 25, 16.
21 *En. in Ps.* 144, 7.
22 *Rule*, no. 7 (ch. 1, 6).
23 Ibid., no. 8 (ch. 1, 7).
24 Ibid., nos. 3, 9 (ch. 1, 2 & 8).
25 Ibid., no. 8 (ch. 1, 7).
26 For example, tribal differences in some nations can present serious problems for harmony and unity in the religious life. In other circumstances the long-established may tend to look down on newcomers (emigrees, refugees) as inferior.
27 *Sermon* 117, 17; see also *Sermon* 69, 2-4.

28 For example: with regard to receiving poorer clothing (no. 30 [ch. 5, 1]) or being too concerned about clean clothing (no. 33 [ch. 5, 4]); the case of a brother who will not sincerely ask pardon (no. 42 [ch. 6, 2]); the true humility expected in a superior (no. 46 [ch. 7, 3]), and not that which is excessive (no. 43 [ch. 6, 3] — here humility is explicitly mentioned).

29 *Rule*, no. 27 (ch. 4, 9.).

30 Bernard Häring. *The New Covenant*. London: Burns and Oates, 1965, p. 190.

31 Ep 6:10-12.

32 *Comm. in 1 ep. Io.* 2, 7.

33 George A Mahoney, S.J. *Broken but Loved*. New York: Alba House, 1981, pp. 30-31.

34 Jm 4:10.

35 *Letter* 118, 22.

CHAPTER 8: *As Those Living In Freedom, Under Grace*

1 *Rule*, no. 49 (ch. 8, 2).

2 Mk 10:42-45.

3 *P.C.*, 14.

4 Bernard O'Connor, O.S.A., "A Call to Reform," in *The Tagastan* 30 (1984) 18.

5 *De civ. Dei*, 19, 14, as translated in *The City of God*, ed. by Vernon J. Bourke. Garden City, N.Y.: Image Books, 1958.

6 *Rule*, no 46 (ch. 7, 30). T. van Bavel, O.S.A., in his *The Rule of St. Augustine* has the following, slightly different translation for this paragraph of the Rule: "Your superior must not think himself fortunate in having power to lord it over you, but in the love with which he shall serve you. Because of your esteem for him he shall be superior to you; because of his responsibility to God he shall realize that he is the very least of all the brethren. Let him show himself an example to all in good works; he is to reprimand those who neglect their work, to give courage to those who are disheartened, to support the weak and to be patient with everyone. He should himself observe the norms of the community and so lead others to respect them too. And let him strive to be loved by you rather than to be feared, although both love and respect are necessary. He should always remember that he is responsible to God for you."

7 *Rule*, no. 49 (ch. 8, 2).

8 *Sermon* 46, 2.

9 Mk 9:35; 10:42-45.

10 *Sermon* 146, 1, 1.

11 *De doct. christ.* 4, 27, 60.

12 *De op. mon.* 31, 39; see also *En. in Ps.*, 148, 6.

13 *Rule*, no. 27 (ch. 4, 9) concerning fraternal correction; no. 29 (ch. 4, 11) concerning secret letters or gifts received from women; no. 45 (ch. 7, 2) concerning transgressions of the Rule itself; no. 46 (ch. 7, 3) concerning necessary admonishing of the 'unruly' and upholding discipline. No. 43 (ch. 6, 3) was also formerly attributed to the superior, but owing to recent research it needs to be seen in an entirely different light. This number 43 does not concern

the relationships of the superior with his religious. Rather it seems to refer to the relationships of all the religious (the superior included) towards those who were considered minors at that time and who were probably not religious themselves. Such young people were often in the monasteries of those times for the purpose of education. Because of their age and perhaps their lack of discipline, it sometimes became necessary to speak to them in rather harsh tones to correct them. It is in these cases that Augustine says that it is not necessary to ask forgiveness, *"lest by practicing too great humility towards those who should be under you, the authority to rule is undermined."* Augustine seems to introduce this number as an exception to the preceding paragraph, no. 42, in which he requires that the brethren seek forgiveness if they have offended one another. Moreover, no. 43 addresses itself to the whole group of the brethren — every verb is in the pural — whereas in all other parts of the Rule, Augustine speaks of the superior only in the singular.

14 *Letter* 78, 8, 9.

15 Possidius, 25, 3.

16 *De correptione et gratia* 15, 46.

17 *Contra Ep. Parm.* 3, 6.

18 *Letter* 22, 5.

19 *De corr. et gratia* 16, 49; see also *Rule*, no. 26 (ch. 4, 8).

20 *De op. mon.* 29, 37.

21 *Sermon* 340, 1. See also *En. in Ps.* 106, 7, where Augustine requests the prayers of his people, since he and they are literally in the same boat together: " *It is the entire ship which is endangered. I say this . . . so that you will not stop praying for us, for you will be the first to suffer from a shipwreck. Or do you think, my brothers, that because you are not directly involved in running the ship, you are not sailing on the same boat?"*

22 See above, chapter 3: "True Friends in Christ"; chapter 1: "Community Life: the Augustinian Experience."

23 *De mor. eccl. cath.* I, 31, 67.

24 *Rule*, no. 44 (ch. 7, 1).

25 Ibid.

26 *Rule*, no. 9 (ch. 1, 8).

27 *Rule*, no. 47 (ch. 7, 4).

28 *De Trinitate* 8, 12.

29 *De op. mon.* 31, 39.

30 Louis Evely. *A Religion for Our Time.* Garden City, N.Y.: Image Books, 1974, p. 71.

31 Tarcisius van Bavel, O.S.A., "The Evangelical Inspiration of the Rule of St. Augustine," in *The Downside Review*, 93 (1975) pp. 97f (April, no. 311).

32 *En. in Ps.* 132, 9.

33 *En. in Ps.* 132, 12; see also *De op. mon.* 16, 19.

34 *En. in Ps.* 99, 10.

35 *Letter* 210, 2.

36 *De op. mon.* 17, 20.

37 *De corr. et gratia* 3, 5.

38 Giles of Rome. *De gradibus formarum*, pars 2, c. 6, as cited in *Const. O.S.A.* no. 31.

39 *De civ. Dei*, 14, 13; *Sermon* 137, 4.

40 Ph 2:8.

41 Jean Vanier. *Community and Growth. Our Pilgrimage Together.* New York: Paulist Press, 1979, p. 128.

42 See above, note 30.

43 Gn 12: 1-4.

CHAPTER 9: *Love The Lord, Love His Church*

1 Amadeo Eramo, O.S.A. *Mariologia del Vaticano II Vista in S. Agostino.* Roma: Ed. Gabrieli, 1973, pp. 1012.

2 *Sermon* 72 A, 7 (*Denis* 25, 7).

3 We have already had occasion to note that the *Rule* does not treat explicitly of the idea of friendship, yet this idea was fundamental to Augustine's view of life, and consequently fundamental also to his view of religious life. See above, chapter 3: "True Friends in Christ," pp. 41-42.

4 The proof of this lies in the fact that he frequently spoke to others of his desire to return to a more contemplative way of life. However, this does not imply that he was slow in launching himself into his apostolic duties. The very volume of his edited sermons and other works of theology already reveal much about his pastoral dedication. (See Possidius, chs. 6, 7, 9, 18, 19 et passim.)

5 Pope Paul VI, who was an avid reader and admirer of Augustine, frequently reflected in his public talks on these two dimensions in the life of this great saint, and on the marvelous balance and unity he achieved between them. For example: "Who was more active than he in the daily struggle for the building up of the Church? Who better than he was attentive to the voice of the interior Master who speaks in the depth of the soul in a secret, continual, loving conversation?" (Paul VI, talk of March 20, 1971, as found in *Living in Freedom Under Grace*, p. 39; see also p. 49).

6 Possidius, 11, 1-5. Possidius was one of those religious from Augustine's monastery who became a bishop; his See was that of Calama.

7 *Letter* 48, 2 (italics mine).

8 *Letter* 243, 8 (italics mine).

9 *De civ. Dei*, 19, 19 (italics mine).

10 *En. in Ps.* 75, 16; *Letter* 132, 2.

11 *Sermon* 260 E, 2 (also known as *Guelf.* 19, 2). For Augustine, even a purely 'contemplative' monastic life has its responsibility. The search for wisdom and truth involves an intense 'activity.' Even gifted 'lay-monks' can and should share with others the fruit of their contemplation. For all this, see Verheijen, *St. Augustine. . ., pp. 22-23.*

12 *En. 2 in Ps.* 30, sermon 2, 5.

13 2 Cor 5:14.

14 *Letter* 21, 1.

15 *Sermon* 46, 30 and passim. The problem of ambitious or indifferent clerics or religious has never been something limited to this or that generation. Pope St. Gregory the Great spoke about this same problem almost two centuries after Augustine, severely criticizing those who

assume the duties of pastors and claim the honors attached to these offices, while they are far more concerned with their own affairs in the world than with properly providing for their flock. (See *Homily* 17, 3, 14, as found in *The Liturgy of the Hours*, Saturday of the 27th Week of the Year.)

16 *En. in Ps.* 126, 2.

17 *In Jo. ev.* tr. 13, 12; *En. in Ps.* 132, 1.

18 *En. in Ps.* 132, 2; Ac 2:42.

19 1 Cor 12:7. These ideas have been reiterated strongly in our own times by Paul VI in his great missionary encyclical, *Evangelii Nuntiandi*: "Evangelization is for no one an individual and isolated act . . . He acts not in virtue of a mission which he attributes to himself or by a personal inspiration, but in union with the mission of the Church and in her name. . . . Nor is any evangelizer the absolute master of his evangelizing action . . . He acts in communion with the Church and her pastors" (no. 60. Dec. 8, 1975).

20 See above, note 6.

21 *Sermon*, 213, 8.

22 *Letter* 199, 12, 46 & 48.

23 *In 1 ep. Jn.* 1, 12.

24 van Bavel, *Christians. . .*, pp. 100, 104.

25 *In 1 ep. Jn.* 4, 4.

26 *De mor. eccl. cath.* 1, 32, 69.

27 *In 1 ep. Jn.* 6, 10.

28 *In Io. ev.* tr. 32, 8.

29 *En. in Ps.* 88, sermon 2, 14.

30 See above, note 9.

31 See *De doctrina christiana*, 4, 15, 32.

32 John Paul II, Talk to Superiors General, Nov. 24, 1978, no. 4, in *Acta Ordinis S. Augustini* 23 (1978) 13. This statement is representative of a thought that has frequently appeared in the Pope's remarks to religious.

CHAPTER 10: *Building Community Through Trust and Mutual Concern*

1 See above, chapter 1: "Community Life: The Augustinian Experience"; also, T.V. Tack, O.S.A., "Augustinian Community and the Apostolate," in *Living in Freedom Under Grace*, pp. 148-157; and "Essential Characteristics of Augustinian Religious Life," ibid., pp. 187-200.

2 *Sermon* 336, 1-2.

3 *De mor. eccl. cath.* I, 31, 67.

4 *En. in Ps.* 99, 13; see also *En. in Ps.* 132, 4; *En. in Ps.* 54, 9.

5 *En in Ps.* 99, 12.

6 *Letter* 78, 8-9.

7 *Sermon* 356, given shortly after the Epiphany of the year 426.

8 See above, note 1, passim.

9 *Sermon* 355, 2.

10 *Rule*, no. 35 (ch. 5, 6); see also no. 18 (ch. 3, 5), where the individual is entrusted with returning to normal observance when he has sufficiently regained his health.

11 Possidius, 24, 1.

12 *En. in Ps.* 99, 11. See also *De op. mon.* 22, 25; *Letter* 31, 7.

13 Possidius, 22, 6-7.

14 *Rule*, nos. 26-29, 45 (ch. 4, 8-11; ch. 7, 2).

15 *En. in Ps.* 132, 4; see also *En. in Ps.* 75, 16; *Sermon* 355, 4, 6.

16 *En. in Ps.* 99, 12.

17 Ibid.

18 *Augustine's* Comment. in 1 Jn 8:10.

19 *Sermon* 361, 1-2.

20 *Rule*, nos. 27, 42 (ch. 4, 9; ch. 6, 2).

21 *Sermo de Cantico novo* 4, 4.

22 *En in Ps.* 90, *Sermon* 2, 1.

23 Rm 12:6; 1 Cor 12:7.

24 *De civ. Dei* 19, 13.